SONINKE WITH OUMAR

Sooninkara Jikke
2023 Edition.

Authors:
Ladji Gassama
Carmen Indrani

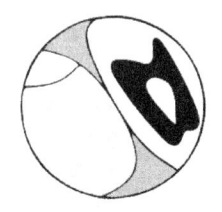

Contact:
sooninkarajikke@gmail.com

This book may not be reproduced, in whole or in part, without the prior written permission of the publishers. All rights reserved.

© 2021 Sooninkara Jikke.
ISBN: 9798388178763

About the book:

This book introduces the reader to the Soninke language through 25 dialogues containing everyday and current experiences through characters from different parts of the world who are part of the life of Oumar, a young Spaniard from Mali.

The book contains a section, **25 Spanish-Soninké texts**, a **vocabulary** section, and a basic **grammar** section. In addition, in the chapters you will find "**notes**" that expand on the content. Finally, you can find the **audios** of the texts on the Sooninkara Jikke Youtube channel, or order them at sooninkarajikke@gmail.com.

About Soninke:

Descended from the Dinga deity, the Old Ghanaian Empire, 10th century Islamic converts, adventurers, traders and corn farmers, some two million Soninke are now settled in **sub-Saharan Africa**, mostly in Mali, Mauritania, Senegal, Burkina Faso and Niger.

For decades, the **Soninke language has been** increasingly spoken in both Africa and **Europe**. This is due, on the one hand, to the growing interest of other multilingual Africans in speaking the language, to the Soninke diaspora that settled in France during colonisation and in the "golden" era of the 1980s, and to new Soninke adventurers (*) with new destinations to settle in, such as **Spain.**

(*) The Soninke and other ethnic groups in sub-Saharan Africa call migration "adventure", migrants "adventurers".

About the authors:

Ladji Gassama was born in 1992 in the **Kayes** region of Mali, into a traditional Soninke family sustained by work in the fields and remittances from migration or, as they call it, "those who make the adventure". Ladji currently speaks Soninke, Bambara, French, Spanish, English and Arabic. In 2018, he arrived in Europe where he began a new journey toward the conservation and care of the Soninke language.

Carmen Indrani was born in 1989 in Seville in the Spanish region of **Andalusia** to a Spanish father, a Tamil-Anglo-Singaporean mother and surrounded by relatives from different corners of the world who filled her life with travels and stories. Today she is fluent in Spanish, English, French, Italian and Catalan. Carmen is passionate about the cultures of Sub-Saharan Africa and has decided to explore Soninke history and culture through its language.

Acknowledgements.

To our family and friends around the world
who always support us in our adventures. A special thank
you to my godfather Bernd and his desire to share his
language learning experiences.

TABLE OF CONTENTS:

Chapter 01. **The Bus Stop**.	Page 06
Chapter 02. **On the Way to Work**.	Page 08
Chapter 03. **Encounter**.	Page 10
Chapter 04. **Chat**.	Page 12
Chapter 05. **Coronavirus**.	Page 14
Chapter 06. **The Mali Package**.	Page 16
Chapter 07. **The Invitation**.	Page 18
Chapter 08. **Breakfast in the Cafeteria**.	Page 20
Chapter 09. **Nora's Birthday**.	Page 22
Chapter 10. **Gossip**.	Page 24
Chapter 11. **Trip to Malaga**.	Page 26
Chapter 12. **Visit to the Garden**.	Page 28
Chapter 13. **Last Day of the Navy**.	Page 30
Chapter 14. **Train Station**.	Page 32
Chapter 15. **In the House of Laban**.	Page 34
Chapter 16. **Film Session**.	Page 36
Chapter 17. **Spanish Nationality**.	Page 38
Chapter 18. **The Super News**.	Page 40
Chapter 19. **Nora's Mother**.	Page 42
Chapter 20. **Freedom**.	Page 44
Chapter 21. **Resilience**.	Page 46
Chapter 22. **Oumar's Family**.	Page 48
Chapter 23. **Dogofiri**.	Page 50
Chapter 24. **Confession**.	Page 52
Chapter 25. **See you soon**.	Page 54
Vocabulary.	Page 56
Grammar.	Page 83
References.	Page 110

Chapter 1. Xaranta 1.

TEXT 1: THE BUS STOP.

Oumar: Hello.[1]
Nora: Hello.[2]
Oumar: Laura?[3]
Nora: No, my name is not Laura.[4]
Oumar: Ah sorry! My mistake. You look like a friend of mine.[5]
Nora: Don't worry, are you waiting for bus number 12?[6]
Oumar: Yes. [7]
Nora: I'm waiting for him too. [8]
Oumar: Ah, here comes the bus.[9]
Nora: Great. Have a nice day. [10]
Oumar: Likewise.[11]

Chapter 1. Xaranta 1.

XUUTO 1: BIISI WUTIRA.

Oumar: Salaamu aleyikum.[1]
Nora: Xa do golle.[2]
Oumar: Kooni, Laura?[3]
Nora: Ayi, ntoxo feti Laura.[4]
Oumar: An faqqu toxo! N toronpe ya. An do n xana yaxare yogo yan baana.[5]
Nora: Ayi, a ma toore. An kanma na biisi 12 ke ya dugu ba?[6]
Oumar: Iyo.[7]
Nora: N ke xá faayi kanma n'a ya dugu.[8]
Oumar: Ah! A kiñanten faayi.[9]
Nora: Heskey. Na kiyen xeerin gabo.[10]
Oumar: Amiina.[11]

Chapter 2. Xaranta 2.

TEXT 2: ON THE WAY TO WORK.

Nora: Hello again![1]
Oumar: Good morning, how are you?[2]
Nora: Fine, what about you? Are you taking the bus today as well?[3]
Oumar: Yes, I take it from Sunday to Thursday.[4]
Nora: Ah! I take the bus from Monday to Friday. I go to work.[5]
Oumar: I am coming back from work. I'm going home now.[6]
Nora: Do you work at night? [7]
Oumar: Yes, I work as a security guard. And you?[8]
Nora: I work as a teacher in a primary school.[9]
Oumar: How interesting! [10]
Nora: The bus is here, shall we continue talking tomorrow?[11]
Oumar: Okay, see you tomorrow![12]

Chapter 2. Xaranta 2.

XUUTO 2: GOLLIRAN KILLE.

Nora: Salaamu aleyikum.[1]
Oumar: An wuyi jamu. Xoori baasi maña?[2]
Nora: Majjamu, an xá moxo? An ni biisi ke ya wuttu lenki xá yi ba?[3]
Oumar: Yebo. N ni wuttu gelli tunkakoota ma xañekoota.[4]
Nora: Ah! N ke ni biisi ke wuttu gelli tuumakoota ma arnakoota. N faayi telle golliran ya yi.[5]
Oumar: N ke giri golli ya. N faayi telle n kaan ya di saasa.[6]
Nora: An gollini wuron ya di ba?[7]
Oumar: Yeboke, n ke gollen ni korosinden ya yi. An xá?[8]
Nora: N ke ni xaranmoxaaxun ya yi, xarallara yogo sappafanun ndi.[9]
Oumar: Adanman ya ni![10]
Nora: Biisin faayi ke dubaane. O na jokki do sefen ŋa xunbane ba?[11]
Oumar: N da mugu. O wa xunbane yi![12]

(*) *Note on the Soninke tradition. The proverb* **"An ga ma siro fantan nagaaniyen falle duŋe ti fogabe kallen ŋa"** *(If you want to be a frog herder you must accept that you will step on some frogs) refers to accepting what you don't like in something you don't want to give up.*

Chapter 3. Xaranta 3.

TEXT 3: MEETING.

Nora: Boy, boy! [1]
Oumar: Gosh! It is you again, how's it going?[2]
Nora: Okay, uh... But, I think it's time to introduce ourselves. What's your name? [3]
Oumar: That's right. My name is Oumar. What's yours?[4]
Nora: My name is Nora.[5]
Oumar: Oh, and do you usually shop at this supermarket?[6]
Nora: Yes, sometimes I shop here after work. Do you live around here? [7]
Oumar: Yes, my house is nearby. It's a 5-minute walk from here.[8]
Nora: Yeah. Well, I like the things they sell here. But I prefer to buy in small shops.[9]
Oumar: Why?[10]
Nora: Because it is important to support local business.[11]
Oumar: What an interesting thing to say! I would love to continue talking to you, but I'm in a hurry.[12]
Nora: I understand. If you want, I'll give you my phone number and we'll continue talking.[13]
Oumar: Perfect. I give you mine. My number is 699... Don't forget to write to me! See you soon.[14]
Nora: OK! See you later. [15]

Chapter 3. Xaranta 3.

XUUTO 3: MEEÑIYE.

Nora: Yigo, yigo![1]
Oumar: Kefaayidé, an ya faayi xadi. An ni kanmoxo?[2]
Nora: Majjomu baane, ehh.... Xaa, n sinmewu ndi dimman kiñe o na me tuw siri. An toxo? [3]
Oumar: Toŋun ya ni. N ke toxo ni Oumar. An ken xá?[4]
Nora: N ke xá toxo ni Nora.[5]
Oumar: Ah! Ken ndi an demi ke taaxe saxan xobeyen ya yi ba?[6]
Nora: Yebo, birenu yi n wa xobene yere golli falle. An daaxan te ni ti yere ya yi ba?[7]
Oumar: Iyo. N kaa faayi tette ke yi, sannu karagi terende ya ni gilli yere yi.[8]
Nora: N da faamu. Yokku beenu ga gaagene yere i liŋ'in ke xooni da. Xaa n ke di bitigi lenmu ku xobeyen ya xerexere.[9]
Oumar: Maniya?[10]
Nora: Baawoni a nafan xooren ni na kundan jaagon deema.[11]
Oumar: Adanman ya ni! N ñ'a mulla nan dalla sefene d'an ŋa, xaa njewe ni fonne.[12]
Nora: N da faamu. Gelli an g'a mulla, n wa mexenkaccenkillen kin'an ŋa, o na jokki sefene ti non ŋa.[13]
Oumar: Eheeyi. N ke wa n xallen kin'an ŋa. N mexenkacinkille ni 699... Maxa mungu nan safandi katt'in ŋa! O wa kattikaane. [14]
Nora: Baasife, o wa falle.[15]

Chapter 4. Xaranta 4.

TEXT 4: CHAT.

Nora: Oumar. It is Nora here. This is my number. [1]
Oumar: Nora! My new friend, how are you? [2]
Nora: Good. I'm preparing dinner. [3]
Oumar: I am on my way to work. I start at 21:30 at night and leave at 6:30 in the morning. [4]
Nora: Do you work 9 hours a day? [5]
Oumar: Of course! It's a job for night people. [6]
Nora: Phew! I like to sleep a lot. At 22:30 I'm in bed. [7]
Oumar: You don't say! Well, it's almost time. [8]
Nora: Ha ha ha ha. Nora: Right. I won't keep you any longer. Have a good night. [9]
Oumar: OK. I really enjoyed this chat. We'll keep in touch, good night! [10]
Nora: Goodbye! [11]

Chapter 4. Xaranta 4.

XUUTO 4: MEXENKACCI SAFANDE.

Nora: Oumar. N ke ni ni Nora ya yi. Ke ni ni n mexen kaccen ya yi.[1]
Oumar: Nora! N xana kurunba. Xori toora nt'an ŋa?[2]
Nora: Majjomu. N faayi kanma na ñaxamen moxon ya sirondi.[3]
Oumar: N ke kiñanten ya ni golliran ŋa. N wa joppana wuron mexe mexe xanne 21h30 ŋa, nan duguta soxuba 6h30 ŋa.[4]
Nora: An ni mexu kaabi ya golli ni koota su ba?[5]
Oumar: Yeboké! Golle ya ni ansiri ti gingin saron ya yi.[6]
Nora: Ugh! N ke xooni wa xenxene buru, mexe xanne 22h30, w'in ñini beren kanma.[7]
Oumar: Maxa ke kon'in da! Ken ndi fonne ta an soxu biren na kiñe.[8]
Nora: Ha, ha, ha. Enn. N ke ntaxa an diganmuurunu xadi. Na wuron xeerin gabo.[9]
Oumar: Baasife. Ke masala liŋ'in da buru. O na ri gemu mexenkaccen ŋa. Na wuron xeerin gabo![10]
Nora: Arin'o koyimeyi! [11]

Chapter 5. Xaranta 5.

TEXT 5: CORONAVIRUS.

(Oumar's phone rings.)
Oumar: Hey! Nora, how are you doing? [1]
Nora: Good. But I was worried about you. I haven't seen you at the bus stop this week.[2]
Oumar: Yes, I'm sick. I don't feel well. [3]
Nora: What's wrong with you?[4]
Oumar: Well, I have the coronavirus.[5]
Nora: Wow! that is to bad. Did you go to the medical centre then? [6]
Oumar: Yes, I got the test results on Tuesday.[7]
Nora: And how long do you have to stay at home without going out? [8]
Oumar: I have to be quarantined for 15 days. [9]
Nora: And your family is well? [10]
Oumar: Yes, my family lives in Mali. [11]
Nora: Ah! I've never asked you where you're from. [12]
Oumar: I am from Mali. I have been here for almost eleven years.[13]
Nora: No way! I hope to see you soon to find out more about your background. [14]
Oumar: Sure, I have questions too. I'll talk to you soon.[15]
Nora: Okay. If you need anything call me. See you soon. [16]

Chapter 5. Xaranta 5.

XUUTO 5: CORONAVIRUSU.

(*Oumar mexen xollen wa sonene.*)
Oumar: Igo! Nora, xori toora maña.[1]
Nora: Majjomu, xaa n ñin ga noxodusame an da, ke koye su n m'an ŋari biisi wutiran ŋa.[2]
Oumar: Yebo. N xaji ya. N m'in du sellente ñi. [3]
Nora: Mani n'an ŋa?[4]
Oumar: Mantanani, coronavirusun ya n'in ŋa.[5]
Nora: Hey! N dawu warijexa bure, an daga jaarandiran ŋa kenba?[6]
Oumar: Yebo, i da segesegenden jaabun kon'in da gangikoota ke yi.[7]
Nora: Ken ndi, an ni wuccu mannime ñaana kaa ndi ñaani bakke nta di?[8]
Oumar: N nan xawa ñini kow fillin toxxe yi kaa ndi bito tanmi do karago noxondi.[9]
Nora: Kaadunkon xá, xori toora nt'i ya?[10]
Oumar: Yebo. N ke kaadunkon birene Maali ya.[11]
Nora: Anha! N ke me ñi n ga d'an tirindi an boguran ŋa.[12]
Oumar: N ke bakka Maali ya. A wa tintono siino tanmi do baane yi nga yere.[13]
Nora: Kefayidé! Ken ya geni n w'a jikki n'an ŋari falle, kudo na fo gabe tuw an naame ndi. [14]
Oumar: Digaame nta di, tirindindun w'in xá maxa. O na sefe kattikaane.[15]
Nora: Baasife. Gelli an ga na fataaji fo yi inxiri mexen kacce ŋa. O wa kattikaane.[16]

15

Chapter 6. Xaranta 6.

TEXT 6: THE MALI PACKAGE.

(The telephone rings in Oumar's flat.)
Oumar: I'm coming! I'll be right with you. [1]
Delivery woman: Hello sir. I have a parcel for you in the name of Oumar Sylla, is that you?[2]
Oumar: Yes, it's me. [3]
Delivery woman: Perfect. Please tell me your ID number.[4]
Oumar: My NIE number is Y6849...[5]
Delivery woman: Great. Sign here. [6]
Oumar: Ok... Oumar: Thank you.[7]
Delivery woman: See you later. Thank you.[8]
(Oumar closes the door and begins to open the package).
Oumar: Oh, finally, my mother's parcel has arrived, poor thing! She is so worried about my illness. Let's see what she has sent... The traditional medicines, the photos, and... Come on! And there are also African fabrics. How beautiful my mum is! I'm going to call her to tell her that the package has arrived.[9]

Chapter 6. Xaranta 6.

XUUTO 6: MAALI SAMBETI.

(Oumar kuraadun kuraadun guranŋe wa sonene.)
Oumar: N faayi riini! N w'a ŋuñini saasa.[1]
Tuncindaana: Xa kira xirise. N do sambeti yogo ri ti Oumar Sylla toxon ŋa. An ya ni ba? [2]
Oumar: Yebo, n ke ya ni.[3]
Tuncindaana: Eheeyi. Faqqutoxo, an yaaxaran kaahitin jaatun kon'in da.[4]
Oumar: N ke NIEn jaatu ni Y6849...[5]
Tuncindaana: Asahanté. An kitti batten ro yere.[6]
Oumar: Iyo... Nuwaari.[7]
Tuncindaana: O wa falle. Nuwaari.[8]
(Oumar da raqen texe na sambeti ŋuñiyen joppa.)
Oumar: Ah! Legerun ŋa, n maa sambetin kiñe. An nta tampini yo! Ke nexodusameye su njangiro ke da. Dugu n n'a faayi a ga da kebe wara riini.... Fatanbinnin yittu, sirofu kaawanto, a do.... Kefayidé! Do fatanbinnira begin yiraamun xá wa di. Ke fooro yaxare xooni dé! N faayi telle a xiri na kon'a da nanti sambetinun kiñe.[9]

Chapter 7. Xaranta 7.

TEXT 7: THE INVITATION.

(Nora's phone rings.)
Oumar: Nora, it's me. [1]
Nora: Oumar, how are you? [2]
Oumar: I wanted to call you to tell you that I can now live a normal life. I am cured. [3]
Nora: I'm so glad! I was just thinking of calling you. [4]
Oumar: Really? Why? [5]
Nora: Because next Saturday is my birthday, and I wanted to invite you. [6]
Oumar: Oh! I'm usually free on Saturdays, what are you going to do? [7]
Nora: Well, look, I'm going to organise a picnic on the beach. Something informal. [8]
Oumar: Which beach would it be? [9]
Nora: The Malagueta beach. I have invited six friends. [10]
Oumar: Great, what time do I have to be there? [11]
Nora: I think around 17:00 p.m. is fine. [12]
Oumar: Do I need to bring anything? [13]
Nora: I'm going to buy a snacks and drinks. Don't worry. [14]
Oumar: Ok. See you this Saturday. Thanks for the invitation! [15]
Nora: See you Saturday. See you there Oumar. [16]

Chapter 7. Xaranta 7.

XUUTO 7: BAASUNDE.

(Nora mexenxolle wa sonene.)
Oumar: Nora n ke ya ni. [1]
Nora: Oumar, xori mantoora maña?[2]
Oumar: N ñ'a mulla n'an xiri kudo na kon'an da Nanti keetanke n raawa bireye moxo siren dabarini, n saha keeta.[3]
Nora: N ñaxali buru! N xá faayi ga ñi kanma nan sinme an xirinden ya yi.[4]
Oumar: Anhan? Ken ni maniya?[5]
Nora: Enn, baawoni tangikoota riiye ni n siinan yillan ya yi, ken do n ñ'a mulla n'an bisimilla.[6]
Oumar: Maxa ke ko! Laada yi n ke tuumana tangikootanun ŋa. An liini mani dabari?[7]
Nora: Eee ken ndi, n faayi riini nellan yigande yogo ya moxon gemundi geeji raqen ŋa. Manqan gabe ga nta kebe di.[8]
Oumar: Kan geejiraqen ñini ken ŋa?[9]
Nora: Malageta geedjiraqe. N bisimillandi menjanŋu tumi yi.[10]
Oumar: Asahanté. Kan mexinxannen xaw'in ñini non ŋa?[11]
Nora: N sinmewu ndi nellen mexe 17h00n siren ni.[12]
Oumar: N do fo nan xawa riini ba?[13]
Nora: N ke faayi telle yigandimisu yogonu xobo do minifo yogonu. Maxa du laasame.[14]
Oumar: N da mugu. Ken ndi, o na gemu tangikoota riiye yi. Nuwaari bisimillanden ŋa.[15]
Nora: O wa tangikootan ŋa, w'an dukku non ŋa Oumar.[16]

Chapter 8. Xaranta 8.

TEXT 8: BREAKFAST IN THE CAFETERIA.

Waiter: Good morning girls, what can I get you? [1]
Nora: I'll have a coffee with milk and toast with cheese, tomato and oil. What would you like, María?[2]
María: I'll have a black coffee and nothing to eat.[3]
Waiter: I'll bring you breakfast in a minute.[4]
María: Well Nora, tell me how things are going, any news?[5]
Nora: Yes, look, I've met a boy.[6]
Maria: Is he your boyfriend?[7]
Nora: No! A boy who is my friend. I met him on the bus that I take to work every day. [8]
Maria: What are you talking about, you're crazy! [9]
Nora: I swear! Besides, I invited him to my birthday. [10]
Maria: That's strong. Well, we'll meet him on Saturday. Are you sure you're not together?[11]
Nora: It is not like that! You are annoying María. [12]
Waiter: Girls, your breakfast.[13]
Nora: Thank you.[14]
Maria: Come on, eat that quickly, we have to get back to work. [15]
Nora: Ok.[16]

Chapter 8. Xaranta 8.

XUUTO 8: XANDI MINIRAN SAAXUBAN YIGAYE.

Taxandindaana: Xa do golle xusu. Axa faayi riini mani yiga?[1]
Nora: N ke wa xande do xati mulla, do buuru biyinte baane do keeso, tamaati do yigete. An ken ni mani mulla Marina?[2]
María: N ke, xandi duuron kin'in ŋa, nta yigande fowofo yi. [3]
Taxandindaana: Saasa, N wa soxuban yiganden beerini xa yi.[4]
Maria: Ayiwa Nora, moxota kon'in da fiinun daga moxo ndi. Xibaare kurunba wa non ba?[5]
Nora: Yeboké, n da yaxanbaane yogo ya tuw.[6]
Maria: Anhaaa! An renmina yigon ya ni ba? [7]
Nora: Ayiii! N menjanŋe yigo ya ni ta. N d'a tuw biisi wutiran ya yi, n ga wuttu nan daga golliran ŋa koota su.[8]
Maria: An ti mani! Ndawu bononté![9]
Nora: Wallayi! Adanfilla, n da bisimilla n siinan yillan ŋa.[10]
Maria: An xá raawa fida. Ayiwa, ken ndi o wa riin'a tuw tangikoota riiye. An sexeyi nanti xa nta doome?[11]
Nora: Don't give them that! An xá moxon xotenni dé Maria.[12]
Taxandindaana: Xusu, axa soxuban yiganden faayi.[13]
Nora: Nuwaari.[14]
María: Ewa, ken yiga karama, o nan xawa nan saage katti golliran ŋa.[15]
Nora: Ewa.[16]

Chapter 9. Xaranta 9.

TEXT 9: NORA'S BIRTHDAY.

María: Nora, shall we put on some music? [1]
Nora: Sure, and then take out the omelette and put it on the table with the other things.[2]
Elena: Maria, what kind of music are you going to play? [3]
Maria: Whatever Nora wants, it's her birthday. [4]
Nora: Elena, help me open the bottle of wine. Oh look! Here comes my friend Oumar.[5]
Maria: I didn't know your friend was African. How exotic! [6]
Oumar: Hello everyone, am I late? [7]
Elena: No way, we've just started. Welcome. What do you want to drink? [8]
Oumar: Are there any refreshments? [9]
María: Don't you want a beer or a glass of wine? [10]
Oumar: No thanks. I don't drink alcohol.[11]
María: Why is that? [12]
Oumar: Because I am a Muslim. [13]
Maria: Ah! Well, it's your loss. [14]
Elena: Well, it's time to sing happy birthday to Nora.[15]
***All**: Happy birthday, happy birthday, happy birthday, we all wish you, happy birthday!*[16]
Nora: Thank you all so much for coming and celebrating with me. I am very happy.[17]
Oumar: I have brought you a gift.[18]
Nora: You didn't have to![19]
Oumar: Yes, it's just something small. Here, open it. [20]
Nora: Let's see... Oh, what a beautiful fabric, is it African?[21]
Oumar: Yes, you can use it for many things. [22]

Chapter 9. Xaranta 9.

XUUTO 9: NORA SIINAN YILLA.

María: Nora, o raawa suuge fonne terinkana ba?[1]
Nora: Yeboké, a do falle an na tortija ke bagandi na wara yige cordommen kanma, a do fo tana be ga non ŋa.[2]
Elena: An faayi riini kan suuge ra yi?[3]
María: Kebe gan liŋi Nora dan ŋa, a siinan yillan ya ni.[4]
Nora: Elena, in deema na viino wordommen ŋuñi. Aaay a faayi! N menjanŋe Oumar faayi riini ti dooke.[5]
María: N ke ma ñ'a tuw nanti an menjanŋe Oumar ñi bakka fatanbinnira ya yi, Ndawu xiide![6]
Oumar: Salaamu aleyikum, N dalla ba?[7]
Elena: A ni kanmoxo! O faayi ga giri a joppa saasa, o wa teŋono! An ni mulla na mani mini?[8]
Oumar: Fo mulle yogo wa non ŋa ba?[9]
María: An nta cerveza yogo mulla ma viinonne yogo?[10]
Oumar: Ayi nuwaari, N ke nta dolo minni.[11]
Maria: Ken xá ni maniya?[12]
Oumar: Baawoni n ke ni silaamen ya yi.[13]
Maria: Ah! Ayiwa, an da du luppandi dolon ŋa.[14]
Elena: Ayiwa biren kiñe na siinan yillan suugu Nora da.[15]
Beesu: *Siinan yilla do soowe! Siinan yilla do soowe! O wa xeerin suusu xann'an da! Siinan yilla do soowe!* [16]
Nora: Nuwaarindi xoore ndo maamanden wa katti ibeesu yi riiyen ŋa, do nan ñaxa d'in batten ŋa. N ñaxalintenni buru. [17]
Oumar: N ke d'an falla muuso yogo yi.[18]
Nora: A ma ken bag'an da yigo.[19]
Oumar: Yebo, fo misu ya ni tanni. Fanŋu a ŋuñi.[20]
Nora: Dugu... Ahh! Kooni yiran faranfare ge ni. A giri fatanbinnira ya ba?[21]
Oumar: Yeboké. An raaw'a ñaana fo gabe yi.[22]

Chapter 10. Xaranta 10.

TEXT 10: GOSSIP.

(Elena's phone rings.)
María: Elena, I can't see you. You told me you were at the corner of the pharmacy.[1]
Elena: I'm coming. I'll be there in one minute.[2]
Maria: Hurry up, I'm waiting for you.[3]
(Ten minutes later...)
María: Your said you were almost here![4]
Elena: Sorry about that Maria, come on, let's go for a walk.[5]
Maria: Well, Nora's birthday was interesting, what did you think of the African boy? What was his name?[6]
Elena: I think his name was Moses, Moussa. I don't know. Oh no! Ammar.[7]
Maria: No, it was Oumar! Anyway. I think he's in love with Nora.[8]
Elena: No way, they're just friends. Well, I don't know. The truth is that he's very nice.[9]
María: And he is not bad at all, is he? Well, he is very quiet.[10]
Elena: Do you like Oumar? [11]
Maria: Are you stupid or what, I already have a partner. One is enough![12]
Elena: Well, but you have eyes, don't you?[13]
María: Leave me alone! I'll bet you anything that Nora and Oumar end up falling in love.[14]
Elena: What are you talking about? Well, tell me how you are getting on with your partner...[15]
María: Well, look...[16]

(They continue talking...)

24

Chapter 10. Xaranta 10.

XUUTO 10: MAXANSEFENDE.

(Elena mexen xollen wa sonene.)
Maria: Elena, N ñaaxe nt'an ŋa dé, An t'in da nant'an wa saharigaageran jingon ŋa.[1]
Elena: N faayi kanma nan kiñe ya, sanni baane noxondi n wa ñini non ŋa.[2]
Maria: Asoobe, n faayi kanma n'an dugu ya.[3]
(Sannu tanmi dangi falle...)
María: A ma bono gell'an ga kanma nan kiñe ya![4]
Elena: Faqqutoxo Maria, Ewa, on daga yaaran fonne dabari.[5]
María: Ayiwa ayiwa, kooni Nora siinan yilla ke ñi adanman ya yi. An da fatanbinnin yaxanbaane ke do mani xawa? A toxon ñi mani yinme yi?[6]
Elena: Anxawa a toxon ge ñi Moises, Moussa. N ke faqqqile nta di. Ah ayi! Ammar.[7]
María: Anhaan, a ñi Oumar ya yi. N ti anxawa a jallinten ya ga do Nora batten ŋa.[8]
Elena: An ti mani! Xananu baane ya ni ta. Ayiwa, n ke nta tuw dé. Toŋundi a noxon xulle ni.[9]
Maria: Toŋutoŋu fo bure fowofo su nta yi. Ma? Ayiwa, a maranten ke ni ya nan dangi faqqe ndi.[10]
Elena: Oumar liŋi an da ba?[11]
María: An tuuri ya ba ma mani ni, n ke renmina yigon w'in maxa nan xasu. baane wose![12]
Elena: Ayiwa, xaa yaaxan lenme w'an ŋa xooni. Ma ken feti.?[13]
Maria: Fet'in ŋa sá! A ga na moti a timen wa bakka. Har'i ga na legeri xanuyen ya yi Nora do Oumar.[14]
Elena: An ti mani! Ayiwa, dantexind'in da an ga moxo be yi d'an renmina yigon ŋa.[15]
María: Mantanani, Ehh....[16]
(I jokki sefene...)

25

Chapter 11. Xaranta 11.

TEXT 11: TRIP TO MALAGA.

(Marina has just arrived in Malaga from Seville).
Marina: Hello, excuse me, is Avenida Andalucía far from here?[1]
Woman: It is not far from María Zambrano station.[2]
Marina: Well, I am actually heading to La Unión roundabout.[3]
Woman: Ah! That's nearby. Look, take a left when you come out of the station... Then turn right at the first crossroad... And then go straight on until you get to the roundabout.[4]
Marina: OK ma'am, thank you very much. [5]
(Marina follows the signs to Oumar's house).
Marina: I think it's here. Calle Fermina 42, flat 4ºA...I'll call.[6]
(The telephone rings.)
Oumar: Yes?[7]
Marina: It's me, Marina. Open the door Oumar.[8]
Oumar: How quickly you arrived! Just a moment, I'll open the door for you.[9]

Chapter 11. Xaranta 11.

XUUTO 11: SAAFARIYE KATTI MALAGA.

(Marina giri kiñe Malaga gilli Sebiya.)
Marina: Salaamu aleyikum, faqqutoxo. Andalusia kaanfallinkille ke nan laatu yere yi ba?[1]
Yaxare: Gilli María Zambrano wurufowutira ke yi a laate feti.[2]
Marina: Ayiwa, aramuuruyen yinme di n faayi telle La Unión killinjingon ya yi.[3]
Yaxare: Ah! Ken faayi yere o tette ke yi. A faayi, daga t'an noogen ŋa biranbe an ga na bogu wurufowutira ke yi.... A falle an na xuuse t'an tayen ŋa, killinfetera fana ke yi... Ken falle keeta a suusu ni teleŋoyen ya yi ma'an gan kiñe killinjingo ke yi.[4]
Marina: Baasife yaxare, nuwaari siri.[5]
(Marina jokki do taagumancu ku yi ma Oumar kaa ndi.)
Marina: Anxawa yere ya ge ni. Kaanun kille Fermina 42, kuraadu 4A.... Dugu n n'a xiri.[6]
(Kuraadun guranŋen wa sonene.)
Oumar: To you kanmoxo?[7]
Marina: N ke ya ni, Marina. A ŋuñi Oumar.[8]
Oumar: An kiñe fane dé! Dugu fonne, saasa n w'a ŋuñini an kaane.[9]

Chapter 12. Xaranta 12.

TEXT 12: VISIT TO THE GARDEN.

Oumar: Come on Marina, hurry up! It is always the same, Nora is already downstairs waiting at the door. [1]
Marina: I'm coming! Don't be in such a hurry, we'll take the lift in a minute.[2]
Oumar: Hi Nora! Look, this is my good friend Marina. She has come for a few days from Seville. [3]
Nora: Nice to meet you Marina, we're going to have a great time here in Malaga today![4]
Marina: You too Nora, nice to meet you. Oumar has told me a lot about you.[5]
Nora: Come on, get in my car, I'm going to take you to the Botanical Gardens.[6]
(In the garden...)
Marina: Wow, what a beautiful place! I've never seen such big trees. [7]
Nora: I love these blue flowers - how unusual! [8]
Oumar: I'm very hot, can we sit here for a while? [9]
Nora: Well, but then we keep walking.[10]
Marina: Nora, do you have water?[11]
Nora: Yes, I have a bottle. Here, drink.[12]
Oumar: Girls, as soon as we finish our walk, I'll buy you lunch. [13]

Chapter 12. Xaranta 12.

XUUTO 12: NAAXUNGALLEN KUURANDE.

Oumar: Ewa Marina, asoobe! A n'i moxo ke ya di tanni, Nora wa kanma nan dugundi wiredun ŋa dubaane, gallaqqen ŋa.[1]
Marina: N faayi riini keeta! Maxa xorti, sanni baane noxondi o wa yanqaanansetufon wuttu.[2]
Oumar: Salaamu aleyikum Nora! Yere faayi, n n'an koyi n xana sire Marína yi. A ri bitan jaatu ya ña nan giri Sevilla. [3]
Nora: Bet'alla ge d'o koyimeyi Marina! O wa lenki dangindini jomu di Malaga yere![4]
Marina: N ke xá wa kundun ŋa Nora, an tuwiyen liŋ'in da. Oumar d'an kon'in da siri.[5]
Nora: Ewa, xa ro n wurufo ndi, ndo xa faayi telle Botánico Naaxungalle ke ya di.[6]
(Naaxungalle ke noxo ndi...)
Oumar: Iyeee! Ndawu ke dingira faranfare! N ma ñi nga da itti dinka baraxate ŋari kundu.[7]
Nora: Ke fuugi bulanma liŋ'in da buru. Ndawu duudanfo![8]
Oumar: Jeberen ya faay'in ke yi, o raawa fonne taaxunu yere yi ba?[9]
Nora: Ayiwa, xaa falle o na jokki do terenden ŋa.[10]
Marina: Nora, ji w'an maxa ba?[11]
Nora: Yebo, wordomme baane w'in maxa. A raga, mini.[12]
Oumar: Xusu, biranbe o ga na duguta yaarana, n wa xa bisimillana saamariyen ŋa.[13]

29

Chapter 13. Xaranta 13.

TEXT 13: LAST DAY OF MARINA.

Oumar: I'm back![1]
Marina: How was work? [2]
Oumar: Good, but I am tired. How was your day? What time did you get up?[3]
Marina: I got up at 11:00. And then I had breakfast like a queen. [4]
Oumar: You really know how to live! [5]
Marina: What is you new morning schedule like? Better that working at night? [6]
Oumar: Yes, much better, now I can use my afternoons to do things. [7]
Marina: Things like what? Meeting Nora? [8]
Oumar: Ha, ha, ha, ha, what a thing to say! [9]
Marina: Well, today is my last day in Malaga, what are we going to do? [10]
Oumar: First, let's eat. I am starving.[11]
Marina: You're lucky, I've prepared some delicious lentils for you.[12]
Oumar: Let's eat! Then we will go to the centre.[13]
Marina: Ok. But before we go, I'm going to pack my bag and clean the room.[14]
Oumar: Don't worry about the room. I'll clean it tomorrow. [15]

Chapter 13. Xaranta 13.

XUUTO 13: MARINA KOOTA LEGERE.

Oumar: N ke saage yinme wo![1]
Marina: Golliran moxo?[2]
Oumar: Majjomu, tampiye tampiye. An kira kanmoxo? An giri kanbire?[3]
Marina: N giri mexen tanmun do baane. Ken falle, n saaxuban yige xoyi tunka yaxare. [4]
Oumar: An wa bireye moxo siren tu dé![5]
Marina: An xunbane golliñan biru kurunbo ku ni kanmoxo? Anfasu dina wurun gollen ŋa ba?[6]
Oumar: Yebo, anfase yi buru, saasa n raawa moonikene nellu ŋa kudo na fiinu yogonu dabari.[7]
Marina: Fiinu xoyi mani? Nan toxi do Nora batten ŋa?[8]
Oumar: Ha, ha, ha, ha, mani fi n'an maxa na koni![9]
Marina: Ayiwa, lenki ni nkoota legeren ya yi Malaga, o na mani dabarini?[10]
Oumar: A fo fana, saamariye. N kara dullen maxa.[11]
Marina: Warijexen w'an ŋa dé, n da lenteja siresire moxon sirond'an da.[12]
Oumar: On daga yige! Falle o na bogu katti debinoxo ŋa.[13]
Marina: Iyo. xaa saadi o billa daga, n faayi riini sarajallon moxon sirondi do na kompen sella.[14]
Oumar: Max'an du noxodusama kompe ke da. Xunbane n ke w'a sellana. [15]

Chapter 14. Xaranta 14.

TEXT 14: TRAIN STATION.

Marina: Hello, can you tell me the train timetables from Malaga to Seville for today?[1]
Vendor: There is a train at 12:00, another at 17:00 and the last one around 20:00.[2]
Marina: OK, give me a ticket for the 12:00 o'clock train. [3]
Vendor: Round trip?[4]
Marina: No, one way. How much does it cost?[5]
Vendor: It's 40 euros. [6]
Marina: My goodness, how expensive trains are in Spain![7]
Vendor: I know; do you want to pay by card or cash?[8]
Marina: By card please.[9]
Vendor: Swipe your card here. Do you want a receipt? [10]
Marina: No thanks, which way is it?[11]
Vendor: Track 12. You have to be on the track half an hour earlier. [12]
Marina: Thank you very much, is there a bathroom here?[13]
Vendor: Yes, at the back on the left. But you have to pay 50 cents.[14]
Marina: OMG! The price of the train, the bathroom fee, they're going to leave me poor![15]
Vendor: Girl, it's the modern world. Get used to it. [16]
Marina: Yeah, yeah. Well, see you later.[17]

Chapter 14. Xaranta 14.

XUUTO 14: TERE WUTIRA.

Marina: Salaamu aleyikum. An raaw'in tuwindini Malaga lenki teru ku mexen xannun ŋa ba katti Sevilla?[1]
Gaagandaana: Tere baane wa non mexen 12h00n bire ŋa, fotana katti mexen 17h00n bire do legere mexen 20h00 naxaanu kudi.[2]
Marina: Baasife, mexen 12h00n biye baane kin'in ŋa.[3]
Gaagandaana: Daganansaageyen ya ni ba?[4]
Marina: Ayi, nan daga baane. A genme mannime yi?[5]
Gaagandaana: Tannaxate eronu ya ni.[6]
Marina: Haayi n ke maa yi sá! Ndawu Españi terun jonkon xotenni![7]
Gaagandaana: Ken tuwinten ya ni. An ni mulla na tuga ti xaalisinkartin ya yi ma xaalisixulle?[8]
Marina: Ti xaalisin kartin ŋa dudaaxoto.[9]
Gaagandaana: An kartin xolle ke soxondi yere. An wa seeda dere mulla ba?[10]
Marina: Ayi nuwaari. Kan kille ni?[11]
Gaagandaana: Killi 12. An nan xawa ñini non ŋa leeri taxande kaane.[12]
Marina: Nuwaari ya dé. Jooxe wa yere ba?[13]
Gaagandaana: Yebo, ma yinme ke yi an nooge ndi. Xaa an nan xawa na tankarage santimu ya tuga.[14]
Marina: Ohuu! Teren do jooxen naxa faayi riin'in ña misikiine ŋa![15]
Gaagandaana: Xusunne, dunaanlegeren ya ni. Dudaa demundi.[16]
Marina: Ken ya ni ké. O wa fail.[17]

Chapter 15. Xaranta 15.

TEXT 15: AT LABAN'S HOUSE.

Oumar: Shall I go up?[1]
Laban: Yes, come up, I'm cooking. [2]
Oumar: Hello Laban, my friend![3]
Laban: Hello! Such a long time. [4]
Oumar: Yes, I haven't seen you for a long time. Almost two months. How is everything?[5]
Laban: As usual, working, the gym and not much else. [6]
Oumar: Mmm, that smells good, what are you cooking?[7]
Laban: "Saga-saga" with rice. [8]
Oumar: Ah! I love it, it's my favourite Malian food. [9]
Laban: I know... You love the sauce because it has a lot of spinach in it![10]
Oumar: What do you have to drink?[11]
Laban: I have pineapple or orange juice. Take whatever you want from the fridge. Well, what about you?[12]
Oumar: I have met a girl I like very much.[13]
Laban: Really? Since when?[14]
Oumar: Almost 2 months ago.[15]
Laban: Ah! Is that why you hardly ever call me to meet anymore?[16]
Oumar: No Laban! That's not why. She is just a friend.[17]
Laban: He, he, he, he, just kidding.[18]
Oumar: The truth is that I am meeting her tomorrow. [19]
Laban: Oops, oops, now you're talking. [20]

34

Chapter 15. Xaranta 15.

XUUTO 15: LABAN KAA NDI.

Oumar: N nan setu ba?[1]
Laban: Yebo setu, n faayi kanma nan sore ya.[2]
Oumar: Salaamu aleyikum Laban, n ke yinme menjanŋe.[3]
Laban: W'aleykumu salaamu! Ndawu faameye. [4]
Oumar: Yeboké, a wuccen dalla naañi nt'an ŋalla. Awa katti xasu filli ya. Xori mantoora nta non?[5]
Laban: Mantanani moxo baane ke ya ni, gollini, fataadu wasene, do fi misu tananu.[6]
Oumar: Mmm, ndawu timiliŋe! An faayi kanma na mani xa soro?[7]
Laban: "Saga-saga" kefini maaron ŋa. [8]
Oumar: Ah! A gem'in ŋa, ken ni nMaali liŋun yiganden ya yi.[9]
Laban: N wotu nan xasu wo... Maxafo ken liŋ'an da baawoni derixayen gaben woyi![10]
Oumar: Kan minifo n'an maxa?[11]
Laban: Jabiiben jin w'in maxa do lemburu. Kebe gan liŋ'an da a wutu firigon di. Ayiwa, an ni mani dantexini?[12]
Oumar: N da xuso yogo ya tu a ga d'in saga moxosiri. [13]
Laban: Anhaa! Gelli kanbire? [14]
Oumar: Ken ŋa tintono xasu filli ya.[15]
Laban: Ahh! Ken yan sigi keeta an t'in xilli, kudo na me ŋari?[16]
Oumar: Ayi ken feti Laban! Ken ma sigi. A ken ni xana yaxare ya ta.[17]
Laban: Ha, ha, ha, ha, n faayi sangana.[18]
Oumar: Toŋundi hari xunbane n d'a wa me ŋalla.[19]
Laban: Uyyy, ken di o na ri masala.[20]

35

Chapter 16. Xaranta 16.

TEXT 16: FILM SESSION.

Oumar: Hello, two tickets for the film "Adú".[1]
Man: Very well. It's 14 euros. [2]
Nora: Shall I give you money Oumar?[3]
Oumar: No, don't worry, I want to invite you.[4]
Nora: Thank you, but as I really like coming to the Cervantes cinema, another day we'll come and I'll invite you. [5]
Oumar: OK. [6]
Nora: Which cinema room is it?[7]
Oumar: Here it says room 10. Do you want us to buy popcorn or something?[8]
Nora: Yes, I want to buy sweets.[9]
Oumar: I prefer to eat salty food. I'm going to buy peanuts. [10]

Nora: Ok. In 5 minutes we have to go into the room, because the film starts. [11]
Oumar: Let's go and buy quickly then.[12]
(After the film)
Nora: The film had some unrealistic parts. [13]
Oumar: Yes, but in the end it's a film that everyone has to like.[14]
Nora: Yeah, if there's no action, people get bored. [15]
Oumar: Can we continue the discussion over a drink? [16]
Nora: Come on, let's go to a bar. [17]

Chapter 16. Xaranta 16.

XUUTO 16: SIINAMANKAAN JANJO.

Oumar: Xa do golle, rowano filli kudo na Adu filimun faayi.[1]
Igo: Iyo. Kun ni euros tanmu do naxato ya yi. [2]
Nora: N na xaalisin kin'an ŋa ba Oumar?[3]
Oumar: Ayi, maxa du noxodusama, n wa mulla n'an bisimilla.[4]
Nora: Nuwaari, xaa xoyi ciinama Cervantes ke riiye nan liŋ'in ke da buru, koota tana o ga na ri n ke n'a tuga. [5]
Oumar: Baasife.[6]
Nora: Kan waranda ni? [7]
Oumar: Waranda tanmundin faayi yere. An wa mulla o na palomita yogo xobo ba ma fo tana?[8]
Nora: Yebo, n wa mulla na mantu yogonu xobo. [9]
Oumar: N ke xooni da sappin man ya yigeyen fasa yi. N faayi riini tigan xobo.[10]
Nora: Iyo. Sannu karagi noxondi o nan xawa roono warandan ndi, baawoni filimun wa joppene.[11]
Oumar: Ken ga na yi on dag'a xobo karama.[12]
(Filimun ñeme falle.)
Nora: Filimu ke kaara yogo wa non heskey ya ni tanni.[13]
Oumar: Yebo, xaa toŋundi filimu ya ni a gan xawa nan liŋi ibesu da.[14]
Nora: A faami, ñangolle ga nta non, saron diixini ya. [15]
Oumar: O raawa jokki n'a jangabono, n'o toxo minni ba?[16]
Nora: Ewa, on daga katti minira yogo yi.[17]

Chapter 18. Xaranta 18.

TEXT 18: THE SUPER NEWS.

Nora: Oumar?[1]
Oumar: Yes, it's me. How are you?[2]
Nora: Good. I haven't heard from you for several days. [3]
Oumar: Yes, I have been busy. But today I have super news.[4]
Nora: Oh, yeah? What's up?[5]
Oumar: I am now Spanish![6]
Nora: Pardon?[7]
Oumar: Well, I've been granted with a Spanish nationality. [8]
Nora: Congratulations, and how has your situation changed?[9]
Oumar: Before, I had a residence permit and now I have a DNI. This allows me to travel easily around the world. [10]
Nora: Ah! I understand... But how old are you?[11]
Oumar: I am 31 years old, and I came to Spain when I was 20. And you, how old are you?[12]
Nora: I'm 31 too! By the way, are you going to celebrate the nationality situation?[13]
Oumar: Of course, on the 27th of May I am going to hold a party.[14]
Nora: Oh great! Let me know the time and place later. [15]
Oumar: Don't worry, I'll send you the information. Hugs![16]
Nora: Take care of yourself. Bye. [17]

Chapter 18. Xaranta 18.

XUUTO 18: MUUSUNANGAARA.

Nora: Oumar?[1]
Oumar: Yebo, n ke ya ni. Xoritoora nt'an ŋa? [2]
Nora: Majjomu. A da wucce baga nt'an fowofo su xala yi. [3]
Oumar: Yebo, n ñi kanma na fiinu yogonu ya dabari. Xaa lenki muusunangaara liŋe liŋe w'in maxa.[4]
Nora: Anhaa! Manin saare?[5]
Oumar: N ke ña españoli ŋa keeta![6]
Nora: An you?[7]
Oumar: Mantanani, i ga da españi saarikaahitin kin'in ŋa. [8]
Nora: Kefayidé! Taare taare! Iyo an xibaarun yelime kanmoxo?[9]
Oumar: Gannin ŋa, taaxen duŋeyen kaahitin ya ñ'in maxa xaa saasa DNI'n ya n'in maxa. Ken w'in wasana nan yaara do dunaa yi ti nowoyen fataaman ŋa. [10]
Nora: N di faamu... Xaa, an ken ni siino mannime yi? [11]
Oumar: N ni tanjikke do siina baane ya yi, n li españi n'in toxo tanpille siine yi. An ken xá, an ni siino mannime yi? [12]
Nora: N ke xá ni tanjikke siine ya! Digandofonde yi, an wa riini saari kaahiti ke ñaxa ba? [13]
Oumar: Digaame xawa ken ndi, jimini fana xason bita tanpille do ñeerundin koota n wa riini ñaxa yogo dabari. [14]
Nora: Heskey! An n'a leeren kon'in da falle ad'a dingira.[15]
Oumar: Maxa du noxodusama, N wa riini a fiiduxullen wara katt'an ŋa. O na me sumbu yigo![16]
Nora: An du koroosi siri. N'o koyimey.[17]

Chapter 19. Xaranta 19.

TEXT 19: NORA'S MOTHER.

Nora: This is the Indian restaurant my mother wanted me to try. Come on, let's go in.[1]

Mother: Well, let's see what the food is like here. You know that Indian restaurants in Spain adapt their food to the taste of the locals.[2]

Elena: I was in India last year, were you born in India?[3]

Mother: No. I was born in Sri Lanka.[4]

Elena: Ah, they speak Singala there, don't they?[5]

Mother: Many languages are spoken; our family belongs to the Tamil ethnicity. Tamils are mainly found in southern India and northern Sri Lanka.[6]

Nora: The country has changed a lot since the end of the civil war in 2009.[7]

Elena: And what do you eat in Sri Lanka?[8]

Mother: The food is very good. You can eat many kinds of curry: lentil curry, fish curry, meat curry....[9]

Nora: Well, let's order since I'm hungry.[10]

Mother: Do you know what you want?[11]

Elena: I do. I'll call the waiter.[12]

Nora: Wait, wait, I haven't looked at the menu. Give me one minute.[13]

Chapter 19. Xaranta 19.

XUUTO 19: NORA MA.

Nora: Ke ni endi saamarira kebe nga ñ'a mulla n maa na temu. Ewa o faayi riini ro ya.[1]
Saaxe: Ayiwa o faayi riini a faayi yere yiganden ga moxobe. An ken yinme wotu nanti españ Endu saamariranu ku ni yigandun gemundini taaxen saron liŋun ya yi.[2]
Elena: N ke ñi endi yeru. An ken saare Endi ya ba?[3]
Saaxe: Ayi. N ke saare Sri lanka ya yi.[4]
Elena: Singalan wa koni ni non ŋa ba ma ma?[5]
Saaxe: Xanni gabe wa konni, o ku kaadunkon xille ni Tamilin ya yi. Tamili nu ku kite ku ne biccati Endi kiyenxenna banŋe ke di do katti Sri lanka kiyenbakka banŋe ke yi.[6]
Nora: Jamaanen yelime buru gelli jamaanen lenmun balaawun ga ñeme siine 2009.[7]
Elena: Iyo manin yigene Sri Lanka yi?[8]
Saaxe: Non ŋa yigandu nan fasu siri. An raawa Endun maxafo dambe gabe yigana: xoyi misaale di Lenteja, Ñexe, Tiye.[9]
Nora: Ayiwa, o faayi riini a muuru dubaane, n ti dullen ya faay'in ke yi.[10]
Saaxe: Xa wotu xa ga kebe mulla ba?[11]
Elena: N ke wotu. N faayi riini yigandi beeraanan gangu.[12]
Nora: Tarinke, dugu n ti n ke ma kartin faayi fina. Sanni baane kin'in ŋa.[13]

43

Chapter 20. Xaranta 20.

TEXT 20: FREEDOM.

Laban: Guys, I think it's time for Oumar to give a speech.[1]
Guillermo: Come on Oumar! Everybody come here. [2]
Oumar: First of all, thank you all for coming. It is very important for me to share this moment with you. Now that I have a Spanish nationality, it will be much easier for my mother to come and visit me. I am really looking forward to meeting her! For all these reasons, I am very happy to celebrate. [3]
Laban: Of course Oumar! We are with you through thick and thin. [4]
Guillermo: Now you can go to the city of your dreams, right?[5]
Oumar: Which one, New York? [6]
Guillermo: Yes, you were always talking about New York when you arrived.[7]
Oumar: Yes, but since I've discovered that there are more places, it's not so important to go there.[8]
Laban: Of course, being free and being able to choose what we want in life is a priority. And Africans don't have these rights.[9]
Guillermo: Oppressed countries are also to be found in America, in Asia. In short, an endless list. [10]
Cecilia: Of course, America. People confuse the United States with the American continent. America has at least 35 countries! [11]
Nora: How unfair we make the world! Because I was born in Spain, I can go wherever I want without giving many explanations. [12]
Cecilia: Let's toast for freedom! [13]
Everybody. Hurray to freedom!
Guillermo: Come on now, everybody, let's dance![14]

Chapter 20. Xaranta 20.

XUUTO 20: YINMAKITAAXU.

Laban: Yaxanbaanu, anxawa biren ga kiñe Oumar na moxotakonne dabari.[1]
Guillermo: Ewa Oumar! Axa suusu nalli yere.[2]
Oumar: A fo fana, ibesun nuwaari taanunden ŋa. N ke danŋa a nafan xooren ya ni ni ni ke wucce dangindi do xa batten ŋa. Saasa españi saarikaahitin w'in maxa keeta, a wa riini newo siri xadi n maa nan keti riini kuurandi. N ke jelintenni xa d'a na me tuw! Ken suusu xanne maxa, N ñaxalinte xoorenni a ñaxanden ŋa.[3]
Laban: Digaame xawa ken ndi Oumar. O ku wa d'an ŋa.[4]
Guillermo: Saasake an raawa telle an liŋun deben ŋa. Ken ya fe ba? [5]
Oumar: Kan ni ken ŋa, Niwu Yorku? [6]
Guillermo: Yebo, biresu an ñi sefene ti Niw Yorku yi an kiñe bire ke yi. [7]
Oumar: Yebo, xaa gelli n ge da tuw nanti dingira tanaanu wa non ŋa, nafa xoore ntax'a non dagayen ŋa. [8]
Laban: Digaame nta di. An naañi fataamakitene do nan keti xerexerendini o ga kebe mulla bireyen noxo ndi ken ni kaanan ke ya. Xaa ku faqqu nta o ku Fatanbinniranu maxa. [9]
Guillermo: Jamaanu beenu beenu semben ga ma xooro i wa kitene Amerikin banŋe ke xá yi, do Asi. Digandofondeyi yinme kareye nt'i ñamana.[10]
Cecilia: Yeboké, Ameriki. Saron wa *Etats Unis do Ameriki continent* ku ya xawarinnaaxunu. Ameriki jamaanun roxoye nta dangini tanjikke do jamaanu karagi di![11]
Nora: Ndawu ñengentaaxu ga kanma nan ña dunaa di. N ke saareyen ŋa Españi noxo ndi, n raawa telle noqqu be ga liŋ'in da naañi fatanfansinde gabe nta di. [12]
Guillermo: Xari o na ŋanniye koyi Fataamakitaaxu nda![13]
Ibesu! Na bereke ro yinmakitaaxu ndi!
Guillermo: Ewa saasa ibesu nan lege!

45

Chapter 21. Xaranta 21.

TEXT 21: RESISTANCE.

Guillermo: Hello Oumar! I am glad you are here to support us today with the Colombian cause.[1]
Oumar: Of course, my friend! It's horrible what the government is doing to Colombians.[2]
Guillermo: Well, we are here today in this demonstration to defend our Colombian brothers.[3]
Oumar: So what are we going to do?[4]
Guillermo: We are going to read texts about what is happening and how we feel. Some of us will be singing, some of us will be raising money.[5]
Oumar: Great, so here I am with you.[6]
Guillermo: Thank you.[7]
Oumar: By the way, what a powerful banner you have made: *Enough repression and terror in the state of Colombia!*[8]
Guillermo: Indeed, that's what the banner says. I'll let you know in a moment so you can give us a hand.[9]
Oumar: Whatever you need.[10]

Chapter 21. Xaranta 21.

XUUTO 21: KENDEYE.

Guillermo: Oumar salaamu aleyikum! N ñaxali an ga yere lenki kudo na kitte kaf'o maxa Colombia fitina ke yi.[1]
Oumar: Yigo digaame xawa ken ndi! Jamaaniyinmankon ga kanma na kebe ña Colombinko ku yi a mañanten ya ni.[2]
Guillermo: Ayiwa, lenki o faayi ke murutiyen noxo ndi kudo na o maarenmu Colombinko ku faasa.[3]
Oumar: Iyo o riini manne dabari? [4]
Guillermo: O faayi riini saagandindi diganxuutu ku yi ñangolle beenu ga kanma nan ña ken do moxobe o ga mame. Dantanto wa riini suugu, yogonu wa ñini kafumandini xaalisin ŋa. [5]
Oumar: Asahanté. Ken ndi n faayi do xa yi yere.[6]
Guillermo: Nuwaari.[7]
Oumar: Dugu fina, manne yiran deese dawlanteni xa ga da dabari. *Liixiyen wose ke yi do jamaanen kanne Colombi noxo ndi!* [8]
Guillermo: Gaare ga nta di, yira deesinte ke ni ken ya koyini. N w'an tuwindini wuccinne noxondi kud'an na kitte kaf'o maxa. [9]
Oumar: Fowofo ga non a kon'in da.[10]

47

Chapter 22. Xaranta 22.

TEXT 22: OUMAR'S FAMILY.

Brother: Mum, you told me that Oumar already has citizenship, is that true?[1]
Mother: Yes of course, I just spoke to him the other day, it seems that this year he will come for the Tabaski festival or after. [2]
Brother: But do you have the money to come? [3]
Mother: Yes, he told me that he will be able to come in a month. Specially to see his grandmother. [4]
Brother: And what about my trip to Europe?[5]
Mother: Well. You will have to wait a bit. Oumar will see what he can do for you after his visit. [6]
Brother: Well, if you don't help me, I can't stay here every day looking for firewood to cook with. [7]
Mother: Before you go to Europe, it is your duty to do this. [8]
Brother: What worries me is my outfit for Tabaski. [9]
Mother: I'll tell Oumar to see if he can bring you *"a complete"* to wear for Tabaski. [10]
Brother: Mum, I'm going to get the donkey to tie it to the cart. [11]
Mother: OK son. [12]

Chapter 22. Xaranta 22.

XUUTO 22: OUMAR KAADUNKO.

Gide: N maa, an t'in da Oumar da Saarikaahitin kita. Ken laabe siri?[1]
Saaxe: Yeboké, n sefe d'a batten ŋa ken koota su, a nan xawa riini yirigi na baananan salli ma baananan ga na dangi.[2]
Gide: Xaa, xaalisi w'a maxa nalli ba? [3]
Saaxe: Yebo. A t'in danŋa ti xasu 1 noxondii raawa riini. Biccati kudo, n'i maama ŋari.[4]
Gide: Iyo, Mani baanen koni n ke europun dageye ke di?[5]
Saaxe: Ayiwa. An nan xawa nan dugundi fonne. Oumar wa riin'a faayi a ga raawa kebe dabarin'an da kuuranden noxondi.[6]
Gide: Ken ya falle a ga m'in deema, n ke raa nta toqqo yere koota kootan suwa murunde kudo nan sore.[7]
Saaxe: Saadi an bicca daga Europu, an ya sigira ni ke dabarinden ŋa.[8]
Gide: Kebe ga d'in noxodusama ken ni n sallin yiraamu ku ya yi.[9]
Saaxe: N wa riini a kon'a da n'a faayi gelli a ga raaw'an fallana kompile yi kud'an n'a rondi Sallen ŋa. [10]
Gide: N maa, n faayi riini do faren batten ŋa kudo na saretin yetu.[11]
Saaxe: Baasife n lenme.[12]

(*) *Note on the Soninke tradition. The saying "Faren ga na ñ'ibiren ŋa a toono ya" (while the donkey can carry, the donkey farts) refers to the importance of employment for young people, when they can work.*

Chapter 23. Xaranta 23.

TEXT 23: DOGOFIRI.

Nora: So Oumar, what is Mali like?[1]
Oumar: Well, Mali is a country where there are many cultures, ethnicities and languages. [2]
Nora: So, what ethnic group do you belong to?[3]
Oumar: My family is Soninke.[4]
Nora: What languages do you speak?[5]
Oumar: I speak Soninke and Bambara. Bambara is a widely spoken language in Mali. [6]
Nora: And where did you grow up?[7]
Oumar: I grew up in a village called Dogofiri. [8]
Nora: Where is Dogofiri?[9]
Oumar: Dogofiri is a village in the commune of Marekafo. Marekafo is managed by the district of Yelimane which, in turn, is located in the region of Kayes. This region is in the centre-west of Mali.[10]
Nora: What are the regions in Mali?[11]
Oumar: Well, there are 8 regions. Kayes, Koulikoro, Segu, Sikasso, Mopti, Tombouctou, Gao and Kidal.[12]
Nora: Wow, how interesting! And what is life like in Dogofiri?[13]
Oumar: Most of the people are farmers, the young people migrate to Europe, and those who remain are mainly the elders and children. [14]
Nora: And why do all the young people want to migrate? The village is going to be empty![15]
Oumar: Because young people are carried away by past generations who have already migrated. [16]
Nora: I see, and when will you visit Mali again?[17]
Oumar: I think I'm going to go in a couple of months. You're invited. [18]
Nora: Thank you! I wish I could come with you. [19]

Chapter 23. Xaranta 23.

XUUTO 23: DOGOFIRI.

Nora: Ken ndi Oumar, Maali ni kanmoxo di? [1]
Oumar: Ayiwa, Maali ni jamaane be yi dambi gabe do laadan ga noqqu be yi, ken do xille, naame do xanne. [2]
Nora: Iyo ken ndi, an ken ni kan xille yi? [3]
Oumar: N ke kaadunkon ni sooninkon ya yi. [4]
Nora: An ni ni kan xanne konno? [5]
Oumar: N ke sefene sooninken ya di do bambara. Bambaran xanne ke ni Maali huruban xannen ya yi. [6]
Nora: An xooro minna? [7]
Oumar: N ke xooro debilenme be toxon ge ni Dogofiri. [8]
Nora: Dogofiri ni minna yi? [9]
Oumar: Dogofiri ni debe ya nan bogu Marenkafo kafo ndi. Marenkafo xá wa ñimini tambaxaara yi Yelimaane daaxan noxo ndi, kun suusu ga Xaayi danqqaŋe ndi. Ken danqqaŋe xá ga Maali kiyenxennan banŋe ke di. [10]
Nora: Kan danqqaŋu nan kitene Maali di? [11]
Oumar: Danqqaŋu seegi ya ni maali di. Xaayi, Kulikoro, Segu, Sikaso, Mopti, Tombukutu, Gao do Kidal. [12]
Nora: Aaah! toŋundi adanman ya ni! Dogofiri bireyen ni kanmoxo di? [13]
Oumar: Saron fo gabe ni soxaanon ya yi, fonnanxawun wa terene nan daga Europu, kubeenu ga sebetini kun ni xirisun do lenmunun ya yi. [14]
Nora: Manne ya renminaaxun suusu ga mulla nan tare? Ken ni deben duuraaxundini ya! [15]
Oumar: Baawoni fonnanxawun terudunxullaaxu do ganninkon taraano ku ya yi. [16]
Nora: A faami yigo, iyo an saagene riini Maali kuura kanbire? [17]
Oumar: N ke nan xawa riini daga xasu filli noxondi. An bisimillantenni. [18]
Nora: Nuwaari! Alla ga na duŋe n wa riini d'an batten ŋa. [19]

51

Chapter 24. Xaranta 24.

TEXT 24: CONFESSION.

Laban: Phew! I have no energy today. I shouldn't have come to the gym. [1]
Oumar: Laban, come on, half an hour more and we'll go. If you want, we can leave the treadmill and do some weights. [2]
Laban: Good. Then we can have a better chat. I have to ask you about Nora.[3]
(In the weights area...).
Laban: What about Nora? Tell me, are you finally going to tell me that you like her? I've seen the way you look at her.[4]
Oumar: Laban! Yes, I think so. The other day I dreamt about her. The dream was romantic. [5]
Laban: Man! You have confessed. What about her? Do you think she likes you?[6]
Oumar: I really don't know. [7]
Laban: Oumar, if you like her a lot, it's better to tell her. Don't keep that to yourself. Life is too short. [8]
Oumar: I'll see what I can do. Next week I'm going to Mali. There I will have time to think about what to do about this issue. [9]
Laban: Oumar, let's go home! I am tired. Don't forget we have to meet before your trip. [10]
Oumar: Okay. See you. Let's go home. [11]

Chapter 24. Xaranta 24.

XUUTO 24: LAXAMINDE.

Laban: Phew! Lenki fanka nti in di. N ma ñi xawa nan ñi riyaana yi fetedunwasera ŋa. [1]
Oumar: Ewa Laban, mexen xanni taxande tana noxondi o wa telle. An g'a mulla o na wurumasi ke wara o na likkixote ke fonne dabari.[2]
Laban: Ayiwa. Kundu yi o ra wa sefene noweye di. N ke nan xawa n'an tirindi Nora ya.[3]
(Likki wutira ke yi...).
Laban: An do Nora ni kanmoxo yi? A dantex'in da. An faayi riini a kon'in da dubaane nanti a na liŋ'an danŋa ba? N di an faayindi moxon ŋari katt'a yi. [4]
Oumar: Laban! Yebo, n ke xá da ken ya sinma. Ken koota n kuw'a yi. Kuuwi ke ñi xanuyen ya kanma. [5]
Laban: Yigo an xá! An sefe saasa ya. A ken xá? An saxeyi nanti a w'an mulla ba? [6]
Oumar: Toŋundi n'nta ken tuw.[7]
Laban: Oumar, gelli an g'a mulla buru, a siren ni na kon'a danŋa. Max'a toxo an noxon di. Bireyen wucce nan dafu.[8]
Oumar: N wa riini a faayi keeta n ga kebe dabarini. Koyi riiye n wa telle Maali. N wa wuccen kitana non ŋa nan sinme n'ga kebe ñaana ke jere noxo ndi.[9]
Laban: Oumar on daga kaa ndi! N ke tampi. Maxa mungu nanti o nan xawa na me ŋari an terenden kaane. [10]
Oumar: Baasife. O wa me ŋalla. On daga kaa ndi. [11]

Chapter 25. Xaranta 25.

TEXT 25: SEE YOU SOON.

Oumar: Nora, thanks for driving me to the airport. [1]
Nora: It's a pleasure. From which terminal do you depart?[2]
Oumar: Terminal 1. Then I have to check in at counter number 59. [3]
Nora: Do you take a trolley for the suitcases? [4]
Oumar: Yes, I will take two. When I travel to Mali I have to take a lot of gifts.[5]
(After check-in)
Nora: Well Oumar, I have to go now. It's a quarter to. What time does your plane leave? [6]
Oumar: My plane leaves in 2 hours. I like to go with enought time. Ok Nora. So we say goodbye here. Thank you very much again for everything. [7]
Nora: Enjoy your family and the things you have missed. See you when you get back. Have a good trip. [8]
Oumar: Thank you. Take care of yourself while I'm away. [9]
Nora: See you soon.[10]
(From far away...)
Oumar: Hey Nora, wait! Before I go, I wanted to tell you that...[11]
Nora: What? I can't hear you. I'm coming back. Tell me. [12]
Oumar: Eh... Nothing, I forgot...[13]
Nora: Ha ha ha ha, you're so weird, give me a hug! [14]
Oumar: Goodbye.[15]
Nora: Goodbye Oumar.[16]

Chapter 25. Xaranta 25.

XUUTO 25: O WA KATTIKAANE.

Oumar: Nora, nuwaari n'in tunci wurufon di fuurakanpiran ŋa.[1]
Nora: Ken ma toore. An bakka ti kan terminali yi? [2]
Oumar: Terminali 1. Ken falle n ke nan xawa na check-in dabari biro jaate 59 ŋa .[3]
Nora: An wa puusunpuusun wuttu sarajallonun ku danŋa ba? [4]
Oumar: Yebo, n wa fillo wuttu. Biranbe n'ga na yi telle Maali n'do muusu gabe nan xawa telle. [5]
(Check-in dangi falle)
Nora: Ayiwa Oumar, n'ke nan xawa telle keeta. Nellen mexen naxaton naqqasi ti sanu tammi do karago yi. An fuurakanpinte ke bakka kan dimma yi? [6]
Oumar: N fuurakanpinten wa bakka mexe xannu filli noxondi. A na liŋ'in da nan daga a wuccen gemundi. Ewa Nora. On sere me yi yere. Nuwaari moxo siri xadi.[7]
Nora: Nimisi wase siri d'an kaadunkon ŋa d'an ga faama fiinu beenu yi. O na gemu saage falle. N'a ña faaren killen ŋa.[8]
Oumar: Nuwaari. An du du koroosi siri n ke xá faayi ke ni sella ke yi.[9]
Nora: O wa katti kaane. [10]
(Noqqu laate yi...)
Oumar: Hey Nora! Dugu! Saad'in ga telle n ñ'a mulla na kon'an da ti...[11]
Nora: Manne? N m'a mugu. N faayi saagene. A ko. [12]
Oumar: Eh... Fowofo, n ñ'in ga mungu nanti...[13]
Nora: Ha, ha, ha. An laasamantenni dé! An kitten kin'in ŋa! [14]
Oumar: Arin'o koyi meyi. [15]
Nora: Arin'o koyi meyi Oumar.[16]

VOCABULARY.

Below, you can learn everyday vocabulary in Soninke, as well as the vocabulary associated with the 25 Spanish-Soninke texts.

GREETINGS IN SONINKE.

Morning.
An wuyi jamu? (Did you sleep well?).
Majjamu (Only happy).
Wuyiran moxo (How was the night?).
Yaawuri majjamu (Without any problem).
Na xeeri ro kiye ndi (Have a nice day).
Amina (Amen).

The greeting.
Yigo an moxo (Man! How are you?).
Xori toora nta an ŋa (How are you?).
Toora nt'in ŋa (I am well).
Golliran moxo (How is the work going?).
Baasi nta non (Good).
Alihamudulilahi (Thank God).

The visit.
Xa do golle (Good) (*)
Yaawuri xa kira (Good morning to you too).
Kaa dunko moxo (How is the family?).
Toora nt'i ya (They are fine).
Renmunu moxo (How are the children?).
Toora su nt'i ya (They are very well).
Xa bismilla (Welcome).

56

*(*) Vocabulary note. In the morning you use "**xa wuyi jamu**" (have you slept well?). From midday onwards you use "**xa kira**" (you've done most of the day). In the afternoon you use "**xa nella**" (good afternoon to you). For the evening you use "**xa sunka**" (you have spent the night here), the meaning is rooted in the night spent by the "grillots" playing music until morning around the fire.*

The farewell.
Na o koyi me yi (May God bring us together again) (*)
Alla nta o yaaxun faramu me yi (May God not prevent us from meeting again).

*(*) Vocabulary note. Amina (Amen) is used as the usual farewell response. When the person being said goodbye to is living in the same house, "**o wa kattikaane**" (see you soon) is used.*

Blessings.
Arna xa xoorondi (May God make you grow).
Amina (Amen).
Arna hanmira fiinun jaara (May God solve the problems).
Amina (Amen).
Na wuyi do safa ña (May God give us long life and health).
Amina (Amen).
Na o kisi dunaa yi (May God save us from life).
Amina (Amen).
Na legeri moxo sire ña (May God give us a good ending).
Amina (Amen).
Arna gunnen liŋo (May God give good luck to those who migrate).
Amina (Amen).
I ga riini na o sir uñi (May God make them come back well to meet us again).
Amina (Amen).

VOCABULARY TEXTS.

TEXT 1.

English	Soninke
Hello	Salaamu aleyikum
Getting it wrong	Torompaye
Friend	Xana, menjanɲe
Bus	Biisi
Day	Koota

TEXT 2.

English	Soninke
Again	Xadi
Good morning	An wuyi jamu
Catch	Wutunde, wutte
Also	Xá
Work	Golle
Back to	Saageye
Now	Saasa
School	Xaralla
Speak out	Sefeye

TEXT 3.

English	Soninke
Time	Dimma
It is true	Toŋun ya ni
My name is	N ke toxo ni
Sometimes	Birenu yi
Here	Yere
Sell	Gaagaye
I like it	A liŋ'in da
Shop	Jaagundira
Small	Bucinne, lamaane
Prefer	Xerexerende
Telephone number	Mexenkacce
To me	N ke xooni da

TEXT 4.

English	Soninke
I am	N ke ni
New	Kurunba
Dinner	Naxame
Reach	Kiñeye
Start	Joppaye
Nocturno	Gingin
Bed	Bere
Night	Wuro
A lot	Buru

TEXT 5.

English	Soninke
Telephone	Mexenxolle
Concern	Noxodunlasameye
Good luck	Warijexe
Medical centre	Jaarandira
How much	Mannime
Being at home	Ñaana kaa ndi
Quarantine	Kowfillin toqqe
Of course	Tell me what you think

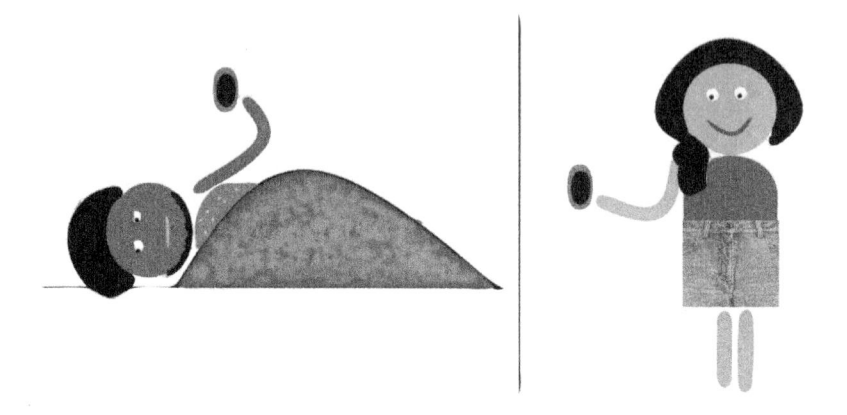

TEXT 6.

English	Soninke
Flat	Kuraadu
Telefonillo	Guranŋe
Package	Sambeti
Perfect	Eheeyi
Please	Dudaaxoto
Number	Jaatu
Great	Asahanté
Signature	Kittibatte
Door	Gallaqqe
At last	Legerun ŋa

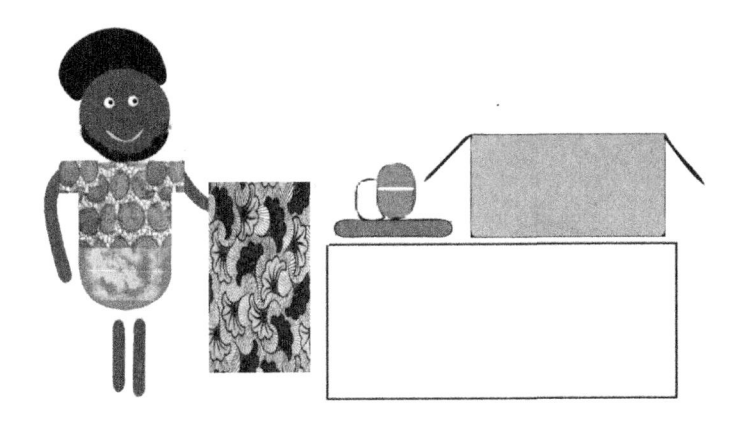

TEXT 7.

English	Soninke
Call	Xirinde
Say	Konne
Life	Birantaaxu
Think	Sinmaye
Ah yes	Anhan
Snack	Nellan yigande
Beach	Geejiraqe
Snacking	Yigandimisu
Saturday	Tangikoota
Because	Baawoni
Already	Keetanke

TEXT 8.

English	Soninke
Girls	Xusu
Take	Minne,
Milk	Xati
Oil	Yigete
Toasted bread	Buuru biyinte
Breakfast	Soxuba yigande
Boyfriend	Renmina yigo
Crazy	Bononté
In addition	Adanfilla
Together	Doome
Also	Xá

TEXT 9.

English	Soninke
Song	Suuge
We can	O raawa
Table	Yige cordomme
Refreshment	Fo mulle
It was necessary to	A ma baga
Detail	Fo misu
Over there	Ti dooke
Only	Tanni

TEXT 10.

English	Soninke
Pharmacy	Saharigaagera
One minute	Sanni baane
Hurry up	Asoobe
Sorry	Faqqutoxo
Paseito	Yaaraŋe fonne
Too much	Dangifaqqe
Tonto	Tuurinta yaxare
Let me	Fet'inŋa
Love	Xanuye
Tell me about it	Dantexind'in da
How interesting!	Adanman ya ni!

TEXT 13.

English	Soninke
Queen	Tunka yaxare
Best	Anfasu
Take advantage of	Moonikeye
For	Kudo
Things	Fiinu
First	Fifana
Hunger	Dulle
Preparation	Moxosironde
City centre	Debinoxo
Formerly	Saadi, Ganni
Suitcase	Sarajallo

TEXT 14.

English	Soninke
Today	Lenki
Seller	Gaagandaana
Around	Naxaanu
Round trip	Daganansaageye
Give it to me	A kin'in ŋa
Mother of God	Haayi n ke maa yi

TEXT 15.

English	Soninke
Months	Xasu
Gym	Feteduwasera
Food	Yigande
Smell	A wa tinmi
Refrigerator	Firigo
Pineapple juice	Jabiiben ji
Favourite	Liɲu
To be found at	Meɲalle, Toqqe
Joke	Sange
Tomorrow	Xunbane
Almost	Tintone

TEXT 16.

English	Soninke
Tickets	Tikku, Biyu
Film	Filimu
Money	Xaalisi
Room	Waranda
Sweets	Mantonu
Peanuts	Tiganu
Buy	Xobeye
People	Saro
Go to	Ewa
Bar	Minira

TEXT 17.

English	Soninke
Good	An do golle
See	Segesegeye
Nationality	Jamaanen kaahiti
Card	Kartinxolle
Good	Ayiwa
Civil servant	Fankamansare
Taaxaana	Taaxaana
Document	Kaahiti
Nuwaari	Nuwaari
Vale	Baasife
Moment	Bire
Quote	Bettamexa
Quite	Wosefo

TEXT 18.

English	Soninke
Various	Gabo
Tidbits	Fimisu
News	Muusunangaara
Congratulations	Taare taare
Situation	Alihaara
Years	Siino
Celebrate	Ñaxande
Great	Heskey
Information	Fiiduxulle
Hug	Me sumbunde
Goodbye	Na o koyimeyi

TEXT 19.

English	Soninke
Restaurant	Saamarira
Try	Temunde
Enter	Roye
Mother	Saaxe
Fish	Ñexe
Meat	Tiye
Waiter	Yigandi beeraana, Taxandindaana
Minute	Sanne

TEXT 20.

English	Soninke
Speech	Moxotakonne.
Go to	Taadunde
Share	Taxandiye
Explanation	Fatanfansinde
Visit	Tuwiye
City	Debixoore
Places	Noqqunu, dingiranu
Rights	Faqqunu
Countries	Jamaanu
Dance	Regaye
Freedom	Fataamakitaaxu, yimmakitaaxu
World	Dunaa
Without	Naañi
Importance	Nafa

TEXT 21.

English	Soninke
Support	Faasande
Horrible	Fomañante
Government	Jamaaniyinmanko
Brothers	Maarenmu
Read	Saagande, Xaraye
Demonstration	Murutiye
Texts	Xuutunu
Powerful	Ketidangume
Repression	Liixiye
Terror	Buttunkutu
Hand	Kitte
Fear	Kanne
About	Dantanto

TEXT 22.

English	Soninke
True	Fi laabante
Grandma	Maama
Visit	Kuuraŋe
Firewood	Suwa
Go to	Dagaye
Bring	Beerinde
Donkey	Fare
Trolley	Sarati
Son	Renyigo
Above all	Biccati
Duty	Xawaŋaye

TEXT 23.

English	Soninke
Then	Ken ndi
Ethnicity	Xille
Family	Kaadunko
Language	Xanne
Grow	Xooreye
Village	Weaken me
Region	Danqqaɲe
Interesar	Fataajiye
Young people	Yaxanbaanu
Migrate	Saafariye, Terende
Elders	Xirisu
Inside	Fonnoxo
Accompany	Leeginde Tuncinde
Where	Noqqube
Still	Harisa

Source: Google Maps (2021).

TEXT 24.

Spain xanne	Sooninke
Energy	Fanka
Running	Wuruye
Chat	Digaamuye
Ask	Tirindinde
See	Faayinde
Dream	Kuwiye
Weather	Wucce
Travel	Saafari
House	Kaa
Thus	Kundu

TEXT 25.

English	Soninke
Airport	Fuurakanpira
Afternoon	Nelle
Aircraft	Fuurakanpinte
Take care	An du koroosi
Always	Biresu
Minus	Naqqasi
When	Biranbe
For	Danɲa, kudo
Farewell	Sereye
Enjoy	Nimisiwaseye

BASIC GRAMMAR.

1. THE SONINKE ALPHABET.

The Soninke alphabet is composed of 26 characters. It contains five vowels: "a", "e", "i", "o", "u" and 21 consonants: "b", "c", "d", "f", "g", "h", "j", "k", "l", "m", "n", "ñ", "ŋ", "p", "q", "r", "s", "t", "w", "x", "y".

The pronunciation is explained below.

The short vowels **"a", "e", "i", "o", "u"** are pronounced as in apple, rent, bill, born and bull.

The consonants **"b", "d", "f", "k", "l", "m", "n", "p", "s", "t", "y", "w"** are pronounced as in bell, doll, fish, kill, loaf, make, need, poor, sit, tool, yat and wet. *Example: bire (moment), debe (people), fene (early), kine (crocodile), leru (pot), mene (cane), na (cow), pine (tyre), sato (water tank), te (oil), yide (axe), wusula (incense).*

The syllables of the consonant "c": **"ca", "ce", "ci", "co", "cu"**, are pronounced as cheese, "ch". *Example: caku (backpack).*

The syllables of the consonant "g": **"ga", "ge", "gi", "go", "gu"**, are pronounced as in gate, get, guide, go, gum. *Example:* guma (stick).

The syllables of the consonant "h": **"ha", "he", "hi", "ho", "hu"**, are pronounced as in half, her, him, hole, hurt. *Example: holo (type of land to cultivate).*

83

The syllables of the consonant "j": **"ja", "je", "ji", "jo", "ju"**, are pronounced as in jam, jet, jist, joke, jury. *Example: jare (stretch).*

The syllables of the consonant "r": **"ra", "re", "ri", "ro", "ru"**, are pronounced as in rat, retail, rist, role, run. *Example: renme (son).*

Sounds specific to soninke.

The syllables of the consonant "ŋ": **"ŋa", "ŋe", "ŋi", "ŋo", "ŋu"**, have a sound that <u>does not</u> exist in English, a nasal sound between an "n" and a "g". Something similar to the pronunciation of the word "gnomo". *Example: ŋana (funda).*

The syllables of the consonant "q": **"qa", "qe", "qi", "qo", "qu"**, have a sound that does <u>not</u> exist in English, a sound between a "k" or "qu" and a "j". It is a sound that is also used in Arabic. *Example: feqe (armpit).*

The syllables of the constonant "ñ": **"ña", "ñe", "ñi", "ño", "ñu"**, have a sound that does not exist in English, a sound between an "n" and a "y". It is a sound that is also used in Spanish. *Example: ñemere (cockroach).*

The syllables of the consonant "x": **"xa", "xe", "xi", "xo", "xu"**, are pronounced like the letter "jota" ("j") in Spanish. *Example: xaso (moon).*

Long or loud sounds.

Vowels can be phonetically used in their simple/short form: "a", "e", "i", "o", "u" or phonetically used in their drawn or long form **"aa", "ee", "ii", "oo", "uu"**. *Example: saane (star), neene (tongue), miimi (the fontanel of newborns).*

Consonants can be doubled in the middle of a word with a stronger phonetic sound. Consonants can be doubled, **"p"**, **"c"**, **"q"**, **"n"**, **"k"**, **"l"**, **"t"** **"j"**, **"d"**. *Example: joppande (start), kocce (stone), yaqqe (wife), benne (horn), sokke (grass), nelle (evening), fette (flea), wujjuune (thousand), fedde (association).*

On the other hand, the consonants "f", "r", "s", "x" and "g" undergo modifications when a strong phonetic sound is required. In this case the consonant **"f"** in its strong form is presented with a double "pp". *Example: kafo (union) → kappe (to unite).*

The consonant **"r"** is transformed in its strong phonetic form into a double "l". *Example: bara (to deny) → balle (negation).*
The consonant **"g"** must appear in its strong form and is presented with a double "k". *Example: faga (to fill) → fakka (filling).*

The consonant **"s"** when doubled is presented with a double "c".

When a consonant **"x"** has to appear in its strong form, it is transformed into a double "q". *Example: joxu (pour) → joqqe (pour).*

Finally, the consonants "m", "ñ", "ŋ", "b", "w", "r", "y", "h" are not duplicated.

Nasal sounds.

The consonants **"c"**, **"q"**, **"k"**, **"t"**, **"d"**, **"g"**, **"j"**, **"ñ"**, **"ŋ"**, **"n"** can be nasalised if they are preceded by a consonant "n". *Example: bonce (to slide), jinqo (hump), kunke (shoulder), fenta (blow), fonde (porridge), mangoro (mango), xonji (puddle), nanñi (to be), fanŋe (river), fonne (little).*

The consonants **"m"**, **"p"**, **"b"**, are nasalised with the "m" although the written form with "n" is maintained. *Example: renme (son), fonpe (air pump), kanbe (tooth).*

The "f", "s", "l", "x", "w", "r", "y", "h" are not nasalised.

Pronunciation rule.

The consonants of a word preceded by a consonant **"n"** modify the oral pronunciation of a word. When it is an **"s"** it is pronounced **"c"**; when it is an **"f"** it is pronounced **"p"**; when it is a **"w"** it is pronounced **"ŋ"**; when it is an **"x"** it is pronounced **"q"**; finally when it is an **"r"** it is pronounced **"l"**. *Example: An saare (you were born). An faare (you messenger). An renme (your son). An wulle (your dog). An xoora (your aunt).*

2. NOUNS

In Soninke, nouns are neuter, i.e. they have no gender. There is a definite and an indefinite form. **Definite nouns** have an **"n"** added at the end in affirmative sentences. *Example: Xa wa xati minni (you drink milk). Xa wa xatin minni (you drink milk).*

The formation of the plural.

In addition, there is a singular and a plural form of the noun. The **plural form** is formed by replacing the final vowel with **"u"**, **"o"** or the particle **"nu"** (in some Soninke-speaking areas with the particle "ni"). *Example: Yaxare (woman); yaxaru (women). Guma (stick); gumo (sticks). Buuru (bread); buurunu (breads).*

Monosyllabic nouns generally form the plural by adding the syllable **"nu"** and lengthening the vowel. *Example: Ji (water); jiinu (waters).* Nouns from other languages also have the syllable **"nu"** added to them. *Example: Kudu (spoon); kudunu (spoons). Matala (mattress); matalanu (mattresses).* Proper names also have the syllable **"nu"** added to use them in the plural. *Example: Gassama; Gassamanu.*

Plural nouns in their definite form also have an **"n"** added at the end.
Example: Woroge (tea); worogen (tea); worogu (teas); worogun (teas).

COMPOUND NOUNS.

The reduced form.

Compound nouns in Soninke are very frequent. It is important to know that the first noun forming the compound noun will be presented in its **"reduced form"**. The reduced form is a reduction or modification of the noun.

It should be noted that in the case of **monosyllabic** nouns they remain invariant. *Example: Na (cow) + xanto (big) → Na-xanto.*
Bisyllabic nouns ending in **"a"**, **"i"**, **"u"** are invariant. *Example: Makka (corn) + biyinte (ember) → Makka-biyinte (roasted corn).*

Bisyllabic nouns ending in **"o"** are normally transformed into **"u"**. *Example: Mangoro (mango) + Xinta (unripe) → Mangu-xinta (mango still green).* On the other hand, there are others that remain unchanged.

Nouns ending in **"e"** that contain a nasalised last consonant **"nme", "nne" or "nŋe"**, or if the noun is at least trisyllabic with a nasalised last consonant, a "real" reduction of the word will be made by ending it in **"n"**. *Example: Turunŋe (hyena) + jogonte (patterned)→ Turun-jogonte (hyena with coloured fur). Alimeti (match) + kaa (house)→ Alimetin-kaa (matchbox).* Nouns ending with the diminutive **"ne"** take the form **"na"**. Finally, the other nouns ending in "e" take the reduced form **"i"**, **"a"** without really a grammatical rule determining this.

THE CONTRACTION OF WORDS

In Soninke, when two vowels meet between words (at the end of one word and the beginning of the next), a contraction occurs. *Example: A beeri + in ŋa→ A beer'in ŋa (bring it to me!).*

RULE OF ACCENTUATION

Some Soninke words are phonetically marked with an acute accent (') on the last vowel of the word for exclamatory emphasis. *Example: Yeboké (of course). Iyoké (yes!). Kefayidé (go!). Ke sirodé (how nice!). Asahanté (great).* Words can be accented in this way in Soninke to differentiate them from their namesakes. *Example: Ma (until). Maa (mother). Má (or). Xá (too). Xaa (but).*

3. PRONOUNS

PERSONAL PRONOUNS.

In subject position:

N ke→ I. *Example: N wa yigene (I eat)* (*).
An ken→ You. *Example: An wa wurunu (you run)* (**).
A ken→ He or she. *Example: A wa telle (he is leaving).* (***)
O ku→ We. *Example: O wa minni (we drink).*
Xa kun→ You. *Example: Xa wa gajaŋana (you fight).*
I kun→ They. *Example: I wa terene (they walk).*

(*) *Grammar note. In Soninke, the particle "ke", "ken", "ku", "kun" accompanies the personal pronoun and is optional.*
(**) *Grammar note. The particle "wa" denotes that the sentence is in the present tense.*
(***) *Pronunciation note. When a consonant "n" precedes a word beginning with the consonant "w" it is pronounced as "ŋ".*

In complementary position:

In→ Me. *Example: A kin'in ŋa (give it to me).*
An→ You. *Example: A w'an terinkana (he listens to you).*
A→ Him, her. *Example: A d'a wasa (she has untied him).*
O→ We. *Example: A di o baasu minifonu ŋa (we have been given drinks).*
Xa→ You *Example: N faayi riini xa tunci (I will accompany you).*
I→ Them. *Example: Xatin kin'i ya! (give them the milk!)* (*).

(*) *Grammar note. When a vowel precedes another vowel, it disappears with a contraction marked with an apostrophe.*

POSSESSIVE PRONOUNS.

N→ My. *Example: N baren dinka ni (my bed is big).*
An→ Your. *Example: An kitaaben roxin ŋa (lend me your book).*
A (another person) or **I** (the same person)**→** His or her.
Example: A d'a ñogomen xobo (she has bought his camel). A d'i ñogomen gaaga (she has sold her camel).
O→ Our. *Example: O d'o kaan sella (we have swept our house).*
Xa→ Your. *Example: I wa xa xalisin kinni xa yi (they will give you your money).*
I→ Their. *Example: A w'i yiraamun yanxini (he washes their clothes).*

THE PERSONAL PRONOUN WITH EMPHASIS.

N ke yinme→ Myself. *Example: N yinme ya ni (I was myself).*
An ken yinme→ Yourself. *Example: An ken yinme daga ba? (have you gone yourself?).*
A ken yinme→ Himself or herself. *Example: A ken yinme tuuma (she herself has rested).*
O ku yinme→ Ourselves. *Example: O yinme d'a faayi (we have seen it ourselves).*
Xa kun yinme→ Yourselves. *Example: Xa yinme yand'a wutu (you have taken it yourselves).*
I kun yinme→ Themselves. *Example: I kun yinme ma sex'a yi (they themselves have not trusted).*

THE REFLEXIVE PRONOUN.

The pronoun **"du"** is comparable once again to an ephatic personal pronoun. *Example: N da du faayi (I looked at myself). A wa du mulla buru (he likes himself a lot). I da du joogi (they have hurt each other).*

THE RECIPROCAL PRONOUN.

The pronoun **"me"** is used for an action between two or more subjects. *Example: I da me fanxa (they have fought each other).*

INTERROGATIVE PRONOUNS.

Ko?→ Who? *Example: Kon ri (who has come?).*
Koonu?→ Who? *Example: Koonun d'a koni (who said it?).*
Manne?→ What? *Example: Manne an ŋa (what happened to you?).*
Minna?→ Where? *Example: N kanjagaane ni minna (where is my rabbit?).*
Mannime?→ How much? *Example: Kaahitinu mannime ni (how many pages?)* (*)

(*) *Vocabulary note. Kaahiti (kaahitinu in plural) refers to paper pages. The leaves of a tree are called yitte dere (yitti deru in plural). "yitte" means tree and plants are called "yitte huuge" (yitti huugu in plural).*

DEMONSTRATIVE PRONOUNS.

Yogo→ Something, someone. *Example: Sare yogo ri (someone came).*
Yogonu→ some. *Example: Yogonu toxi yere (some have stayed here).*

Ke→ This. *Example: Ke ni nfaaba ya yi (this is my father).*
Ku→ These. *Example: Ku ni taalibenun ya yi (these are pupils).*
Ken→ That one. *Example: Ken bure feti (that one is not bad).*
Kun→ Those. *Example: Kun renminu daga suwa (those children went to fetch firewood).*
Kiteere→ He or she. *Example: Kiteeren ni nmobilin ya yi (that's my car).*
Kutuuru→ Those or those. *Example: Kutuuru ni ncaaranon ya yi (those are my parents).*

NUMERICAL PRONOUNS.

Baane (one), **fillo** (two), **sikko** (three), **naxato** (four), **karago** (five), **tunmu** (six), **ñeeru** (seven), **seegu** (eight), **kaabu** (nine), tanmu (ten).

Tanmu (ten) **do baane** (one)→ eleven. (*)
Tanmu do fillo (twelve), **Tanmu do kaabu** (nineteen)...

(*) Grammatical note. The conjunction "do" (and) is placed between the tens of the units.

From 20 onwards the ten is made up of the reduced form of "tanmu" (ten), "tan" and the number of tens made up of the units from 1 to 9 ending in "e". *Example: Tanfille do naxato (twenty-four).*

Tanfille (twenty), **tanjikke** (thirty), **tannaxate** (forty), **tankarage** (fifty) **tandume*** (sixty), **tanñere** (seventy), **tansege** (eighty), **tankabe** (ninety) (*).

> (*) *Grammar note. There are two exceptions to the rule. Tan + sikko = Tanjikke (tansikke) Tan + tunmu = Tandume (tantume).*

Kame (hundred); **kamo** (hundreds).
Wujjuune (thousand); **wujjuunu** (thousands).
Miliyo (million); **miliyonu** (million).
Miliyaari (billion); **miliyaari** (billions).

Below is an example of the rules explained in this section.
Siine (the year) **wujjuune do kamo kabi tansege do kabu** *(nineteen hundred and eighty-nine)* → The year 1989.

4. ADEJTIVES.

DEMONSTRATIVE ADJECTIVES.

Demonstrative adjectives can precede or follow the noun, except "yogo" (something or someone). When "yogo" refers to something, it always appears at the end.

Yogo→ Something, someone. *Example: Yaxaren wa fo yogo xobono (the woman buys something). Yigon da sare yogo ka (the man has insulted someone).*
Yogonu→ Some. *Example: Ittu yogonu wa frigo ndi (some medicines are in the fridge).*
Ke→ Este or esta. *Example: A da ke tere ya wutu soxuba ke yi (she has taken this train this morning).*
Ku→ These or these. *Example: Nta gollini ku koyu su yi (I don't work these weeks).*
Ken→ Ese or esa. *Example: Lo an na na ken cokala beer'in ŋa (go in and get me that chocolate!).*

Kun→ Esos or esas. *Example: N ñ'a mulla na kun tefunu xobo (I wanted to buy those shoes).*
Kiteere→ That one. *Example: N wa kiteeren jaxe gaagana (I sell that lamb).*
Kutuuru→ Those. *Example: O da kutuurun yaxaru kuuñi (we greet those women).*

RELATIVE ADJECTIVES.

Kebe (which one). *Example: N maama Ayise kebe ga faati a ñi a ga xooro (my grandmother Ayise who died, she was very old).* (*) **Kubeenu** (which or which). *Example: Remina dunbu kubeenu ga saare daaru i wa riini toxore Hawa do Adama (the babies who were born yesterday will be called Eve and Adam.*

> (*) *Grammatical note. The particle "ga" or "ge" belongs to the relative adjectives "kebe" and "kubeenu".*

NUMERICAL ADJECTIVES.

In general, numerical adjectives accompanying a noun are modified with the ending **"i"**.

The number 1 remains the same. *Example: Taaxufo-baane (a stool).* From 2 to 10 the noun precedes the numeral adjective. *Example: Taaxufonu-filli (two chairs). Yeliŋu-ñeeri (seven birds).*

From 11 to 19 the noun is preceded by the numeral adjective "tanmi" (ten) and followed by the conjunction "do" (and), and the units from 1 to 9 corresponding to the number. *Example: buurunu tanmi do fillo (twelve loaves of bread). Makkan jogodu tanmi do karago (fifteen corn ears).*

From 20 to 99 the numeral adjective appears before the noun indicating the ten and then after the noun with the conjunction "do" indicating the units. *Example: Tannaxate do faru kaabi (forty-nine donkeys). Tankarage doroke (fifty t-shirts).*

Below is an example of the rules explained in this section. **Wujjuune** *(one thousand)* **do kamo kaabi tansege** *(nine hundred and eighty)* **do saro** *(and people)* **kaabi** *(nine)* **ñi nonŋa** *(there were)* → *There were 1989 people.*

QUALIFYING ADJECTIVES.

This type of adjective uses the grammatical rules of the noun in Soninke. In compound words, the adjective is placed later in the compound. *Example: Kaa (house) + Kurunba (new) + Xulle (white)* → *Kaaxulle (the white house), Kaaxulle - kurunba (the new white house).*

FORMATION OF THE COMPARATIVE AND SUPERLATIVE.

In general, the comparative form is expressed by transforming the last vowel into **"a"**. *Example:* An yaaxo na misa dina nyaaxon ŋa (your eyes are smaller than my eyes) (*) N muusine na dinka dina a wullen ŋa (my cat is bigger than your dog) (**).

(*) Grammar note. The particle "dina" is optional and accompanies the comparative and superlative form.
(**) Grammatical note. In the case of an adjective ending in "a", the comparative form remains the same.

The comparative is also used for the construction of the superlative with a different structure. *Example: An yaaxo ke ya misa dina isu yi (your eyes are the smallest). N muusine ke yan dinka dina isu yi (my cat is the biggest)* (*).

> (*) *Grammar note. "Din'isu yi" marks the superlative form.*

5. THE VERBS

In Soninke there are **phrases without a verb** (noun phrases and adjectival phrases). The essential particle of a sentence is called the "predicative", which will be explained later. The verb in Soninke takes two forms. One form expresses the accomplishment of the action, used for the past and future form, the accomplished form. And a second form emphasises the duration of the action, the unachieved form.

FORMATION OF THE "UNACHIEVED FORM".

In the **first conjugation**, an "n" and the final vowel of the attained form are added. *Example: the achieved form "kini" → its unachieved form is "kinni" (giving).* In the case of a monosyllabic verb, the vowel is lengthened to the attained form. *Example: the attained form "ro" → its unattained form is "roono" (entering).*

In the **second conjugation, the** last vowel of the attained form is deleted, the last consonant of the attained form is doubled and the penultimate vowel of the attained form is added. *Example: its unsuccessful form "setu" → its unsuccessful form is "sette" (going up).*

96

We must take into account the group of consonants that are transformed into their duplicate form. The **"f"** changes to **"pp"**; the **"r"** changes to **"ll"**, the **"s"** changes to **"cc"**; the **"x"** changes to **"qq"** and the **"g"** changes to **"kk"**. *Example: bifi (to stumble), bippi (stumbling). Saxu (to lie down), saqqa (lying down). Mugu (to hear), mukku (hearing)* (*).

> (*) *Vocabulary note. In Soninke when a person stumbles forward "bifi" is used, when a person falls backwards "singi" is used, when a person falls sideways "saxu" is used, also used to refer to the verb "to lie down".*

THE FORMULA OF THE VERB "ESTAR" IN THE PRESENT TENSE.

N ke faayi→ I am. *Example:* N faayi gunne ndi (I am in the field).
An ken faayi→ You are. *Example:* An faayi xaralan ŋa (you are in school).
A ken faayi→ He or she is. *Example:* A faayi yigene (she is eating).
O ku faayi→ We are. *Example: O faayi sefene (we are talking).*
Xa kun faayi→ Vosotros o vosotras estáis. *Example:* Xa faayi yanqini (you are taking a shower)*.*
I kun faayi→ They are. *Example: I faayi safandini (they are writing).*

THE FORMULA OF THE VERB "TO BE" IN THE PRESENT TENSE.

N ke ni→ I am. *Example: N ke ni nagaanan ya yi (I am a shepherd)* (*).
An ken ni→ You are. *Example*: *An ken ni xoodakattaanan ya yi (you are a footballer).*

A ken ni→ He or she is. *Example: A ken ni suxuña ya yi (he is a sorcerer)* (**).
O ku ni→ We are. *Example: O ku surun ya ni (we are nice.)* (***)
Xa kun ni→ You are. *Example: Xa ku dinkan ya ni (you are fat).*
I kun ni→ They are. *Example: I kun ni menjanŋun ya yi (they are friends).*

> (*) *Pronunciation note. When an "n" precedes a word beginning with the consonant "y" it is pronounced as a "ñ".*
> (**) *Grammar note. The post-position "ya yi" accompanies the present tense verb form of the verb "to be" when referring to professions and activities that identify a person.*
> (***) *Grammar note: The "ni" in "ke ni", "ku ni" and "kun ni" appears as a post-position at the end of the sentence in the present tense verb form of the verb "to be" when describing physical and personality qualities.*

THE ORDER OF WORDS IN SENTENCES.

In a noun phrase the order used is:
subject + predicate + complement + postposition.
Example: Birama (subject) ni (predicate) mobiliwurundan (complement) ya yi (post-position). → *Birama is a driver.*

In an adjectival phrase the order used is:
subject + attribute + predicate.
Example: Ke renmine (subject) bucinne (attribute) ni (predicate). → *This child is small.*

In an intransitive verb phrase the order used is:
subject + predicate + verb + verb + complement + post-position.
Example: A (subject) wa (predicate) sorene (verb) juma-riiye (post-position). → *She cooks next Friday.*

In a transitive verb phrase the order used is:
subject + predicate + object + verb (and/or preposition) + complement (and/or post-position).
Example: I (subject) wa (predicate) fattaye (object) mini (verb) konpe (complement) ndi (post-position).

TRANSITIVE VERBS.

In Soninke the verb in its transitive form (when the verb refers to a direct object) is modified from its intransitive form.

Formation of the "transitive form".
Sometimes, intransitive verbs ending **in "e" change to "a"** in their transitive form. *Example: Jaarene, jaarana (to cure something). Sinmene, sinmana (to think of something).* Other verbs in their intransitive form ending **in "e" change to "o" in their** transitive form. *Example: Booxene, booxono (to tear something).* Intransitive verbs ending in **"i" usually change to "u" in their** transitive form. *Example: Kutundini, kuttu (to cut something).*

6. THE PREDICATIVES.

They are generally monosyllabic and an essential part of the sentence. In noun and adjectival phrases without a verb, the predicative determines the form. In verb phrases, the predicative specifies the tense and mood of the sentence by taking three forms: **affirmative** (simple statement of a fact), **negative** (negation of a stated fact) and **emphatic** (questions, answers to questions, and to insist on a particular aspect).

OF NOUN PHRASES:

Definitional predicatives.
Affirmative **"ni"**. *Example: N ni yigon ya yi (I am a man).*
Negative **"faith"**. *Example: Yigo faith (it is not a man).*
Emphatic **"ni"**. *Example: Ko ni? (who is it?).*

Predicatives of relation.
- Affirmative **"ni"**. *Example: Tumaani ni nooxen ya yi (Tumani is very quiet).*
- Negative **"feti"**. *Example: Mamedi feti nooxe yi (Mamedi is not quiet).*
- Emphatic **"ni"**. *Example: Ko ni nooxinten ŋa i di (who is the quiet one of the two?).*

Predicatives of location.
- Affirmative **"fa"**. *Example: Baaba fa i kaara (father is in his land/home).*
- Negative **"nta"**. *Example: Baaba nta españi yere (dad is not here in Spain).*
- Emphatic **"na"**. *Example: Baaba na Maali ya! (dad is in Mali!).*

Predicatives of past location.
- Affirmative **"ñi"**. *Example: O ñi Maali (we have been to Mali).*
- Negative **"mañi"**. *Example: O mañi Burukina (we have not been to Burkina).*
- Emphatic **"ñi"**. *Example: Xa ñi minna yi Afiriki (Where have you been in Africa?).*

OF ADJECTIVAL PHRASES:

Predicatives of relation-attribute.
- Affirmative **"ni"**. *Example: Sii xullen ni (the horse is white).*
- Negative **"faith"**. *Example: Sii binne fe (the horse is not black).*
- Emphatic **"ni"**. *Example: Sii dunben ya ni ba? (is the horse red?).*

Comparative-superlative predicatives.
- Affirmative **"nan"**: *Example: Balaba nan jawu sefene (Balaba speaks very fast).*
- Negative **"nta"**. *Example: Birama nta jawu sefene Balaba yi (Birama does not speak faster than Balaba).*
- Emphatic **"n"**. *Example: Karim ya n jawu sefene kuttu ku su yi (Karim speaks faster than anyone else).*

OF VERB PHRASES:

The grammar contemplates differences between transitive and intransitive verbs, in this book you will be able to see the most used forms.

Present.

Intransitive.
- Affirmative **"wa"**. *Example: N wa tanjini (I urinate).*
- Negative **"nta"**. *Example: N nta gilli (I don't get up).*
- Emphatic (the predicative does not appear).
Example: An gilli ya! (I told you to get up!).

Transitive.
- Affirmative **"wa"**. *Example:* Booren wa yillen soppini (the bird pecks at the wheat).
- Negative **"nta"**. *Example:* Booren nta yillen soppini *(the bird is not pecking at the wheat).*
- Emphatic **"na"**. *Example:* Booren na manne soppini (what is the bird pecking at?).

Past imperfect.

Intransitive.
- Affirmative **"ñi"**. Example: *N ñi tanjini (I was urinating).*
- Negative **"mañi"**. Example: *N mañi tanjini (I was not urinating).*
- Emphatic **"ñi"**. Example: *A ñi tanjini ya! (she was urinating!).*

Transitive.
- Affirmative **"ñi"**. Example: *I ñi kitaaben faayini (they looked at the book).*
- Negative **"mañi"**. Example: *I mañi kitaaben faayini (they did not look at the book).*
- Emphatic **"ñi"**. Example: *I ñi manne faayini? (what were they looking at?).*

Past perfect.

Intransitive.
- Affirmative (the predicative does not appear). *Example: A xenu (he fell).*
- Negative **"ma"**. *Example: A ma xenu (she did not fall).*
- Emphatic **"n"**. *Example: Ko n xenu? (who fell?).*

<u>Transitive.</u>
- Affirmative **"da"**. *Example: N da ngida daro (I have respected my elder brother).*
- Negative **"ma"**. *Example: An ma gide daro (you have not respected the elder brother).*
- Emphatic **"da"**. *Example: An da da manne ña? (What have you done?).*

Future.

- Affirmative **"na"**. *Example: O na soxo (we will cultivate). N na na ji joxu (I will pour water).*
- Negative **"nta"**. *Example: O nta soxono (we will not cultivate). N nta ji joqqo (I will not pour water).*
- Emphatic **"na"**. *Example: O na soxo ya (surely we will cultivate). An na manne joxu? (what are you going to pour?).*

Subjunctive.

- Affirmative **"nan o na"**. *Example: Xa nan gemu (you must make peace). An na ke diganta safa (you have to write this sentence).*
- Negative **"na maxa"**. *Example: Xa na maxa gaja (you should not fight). An nan maxa sare kari (you don't have to kill anyone).*

Imperative + realised form.

<u>Intransitive.</u>
- Affirmative. For the second person singular and plural there is no predicative. *Example: Taaxu! (sit down!).* In the first person plural ("o"). An "n" is added to the latter form. *Example: O n yige (let's eat!).*
- Negative **"maxa"**. *Example: Xa maxa sonxo! (don't make noise!).*

The postposition **"xo"** is comparable to "as". *Example: A faayi terene xo minnaana (he is walking as a drunkard).*

The postposition **"wure"** is comparable to "under" or "beneath". *Example:* Ñiinen *faayi baren wure (the rat is under the bed).*

8. CONJUNCTIONS.

In Soninke we find on the one hand simple coordinating conjunctions between nouns. The conjunction **"do"** is comparable to the conjunction "and" in English. *Example: An do nke (you and I).*

And the conjunction **"má"** which could be comparable to the conjunction "or" in Spanish. *Example: Taye má nooge? (right or left?).*

On the other hand, we find logical coordinating conjunctions between prepositions such as **"xaa"** comparable to "but". *Example: Nagaanan wa juman xatinu minni xaa kacce nta roono na yi (the shepherd drinks Friday's milk, but does not tie up the cows for sale)* (*).

> (*) *Cultural note. This Soninke proverb confirms a social rule whereby herders (generally of Peul/Pular ethnic origin), who work for the owners of the cattle, are entitled to drink the milk of these cows on Fridays, and may refuse to give milk to the owner of the cattle on that day. The rest of the week, the milk belongs to the family that owns the cattle.*

Finally, we find subordinating conjunctions such as **"gelli"** (since), **"ma"**, **"katta"** (before). *Example: Gelli n na kende nsaage do xarannen ŋa (Since I am cured I have returned to my studies). N nta gilli ma xunbane soxuba (I don't get up until tomorrow morning). Yanqi katta jaarandaanan ga riini (Take a shower before the nurse comes).*

9. THE ADVERBS.

The adverb **"xadi"** can be compared to "again", "once more". *Example: Lo xadi (enter again).*
The adverb **"abada"** is comparable to "never". *Example: Fure ntaxa gilli abada (the dead man never gets up).*
The adverb **"duudo"** can be compared to the adverb of time "already". *Example: An duguta duudo (have you finished already?).*
The adverb **"fina"** can be comparable to "yet". *Example: N ma saage fina (I am not back yet).*
The adverbs **"hari"** and **"harisa"** are comparable to "still", "even" or "still". *Example: Hari juma o wa gollini eropu (in Europe you work even on Fridays). Harisa a wa fateduwasera (he is still in the gym).*
The adverbs **"buru"** and **"siri"** are comparable to "very much", "very". *Example: An sirenni siri (you are very kind). A raawa wurunu siri (she can run a lot).*

(*) Vocabulary note. In Soninke, the word "yiriginnu" is used to refer to "several weeks ago". Example: Yiriginnun ŋa renmine yogo bange o debe kedi (A baby was born several weeks ago in our village).

10. INTERROGATIVE PARTICLES.

The particle **"ba"** is placed at the end of the interrogative sentence to emphasise it. There are no direct equivalents in English. *Example: A gille ni ba? (Is he tall?).*

The particle **"n'ke ti"** and **"xori"** appears to emphasise the affirmative phrase at the beginning of the sentence, something like "isn't it?"? *Example: Keeti an raawa sooninken ŋa? (you know soninké, don't you?). Xori toora nta an ŋa? Its literal translation is "You don't have any problems, do you?", but the meaning of the phrase is equivalent in English to "How are you?".*

11. THE PREFIXES.

The geographical origin is indicated by the suffix **"nke"**. Examples: Malinke (Malian), Malaganke (Malagueño), Madridinke (Madrilenian), Indunke (Indian), Singaporeinke (Singaporean).

The suffixes **"ye"**, **"nde"**, **"ŋe"** are attached to the infinitive to form verbal nouns. *Example: soxo (to cultivate), soxoye (culture). Faayi (to look), faayinde (look). Masala (to talk), masalaŋe (talk).*

In soninke the suffixes **"aade"**, **"oode"**, **"aadi"** designate the tool necessary for the action. *Example: soxo (cultivate), soxoode (seed).*

The suffix **"aaxu"** forms the form of abstract nouns. *Example: bure (bad), buraaxu (evil).*

The action agent is formed with the suffixes **"aana"** or sometimes **"a"**. In the plural we use "aano". *Example: soxo (to cultivate), soxaana (the cultivator).*

The suffix **"ndi"** or **"andi"** added to a cardinal number forms the ordinal number. *Example: seegu (eight), seegundi (eighth). Carago (five), caragandi (fifth).*

The diminutive is formed in Soninke with the suffix **"nne"** or **"ne"**. *Example: debe (village), debinne (little village).*

Bibliography.

Breyo, A. (2019). *Je me debrouille en Soninké.* Amazone Afrique.

Girier, C. (1996). *Parlons soninké (*Vol. 1). L'Harmattan.

Jónsson, G. (2008). *Migration aspirations and immobility in a Malian Soninke village.*

Kamps, B. (2015). *The Word Brain.* Spanish Edition. Flying Publisher.

Sylla, Y. (2020). *Le Soninké Pas à Pas.* L'Univers du Petit Africain.

Soumaré, Z., N'diaye, S., & Wagué, C. (2020). *Penser et écrire la société soninké aujourd'hui.* L'Harmattan.

Timera, M. (1996). *Les Soninké en France: d'un histoire à l'autre.* Karthala Editions.

Printed in Great Britain
by Amazon